The Criminal Justice and Mental Health Systems

The Criminal Justice and Mental Health Systems

KENT S. MILLER
Florida State University

CONFLICT AND COLLUSION

 Oelgeschlager, Gunn & Hain, Publishers, Inc.
Cambridge, Massachusetts

International Standard Book Number: 0-89946-032-1

Library of Congress Catalog Card Number: 80-12755

Printed in the United States of America

This project was supported by Grant Number 77NI-99-0061 awarded by the Law Enforcement Assistance Administration, U.S. Department of Justice, under the Omnibus Crime Control and Safe Streets Act of 1968, as amended. Points of view or opinions stated in this document are those of the author and do not necessarily represent the official position or policies of the U.S. Department of Justice.

Library of Congress Cataloging in Publication Data

Miller, Kent S
   The criminal justice and mental health systems.

   Bibliography: p.
   Includes index.
   1. Criminal justice, Administration of—United
States.   2. Mental health services—United States.
I. Title. [DNLM: 1. Jurisprudence.   2. Forensic
psychiatry—United States. W740 M648c]
HV6791.M54   364.6   80-12755
ISBN 0-89946-032-1

Jacket design by Linda A. Fischer

Contents

Preface

In the late 1960s and the early 1970s, much concern was expressed over the medicalization of deviance and the development of the therapeutic state. By the mid-1970s, this concern appeared to be on the wane, although there were some indications that the therapeutic state was continuing to advance in more subtle form. Upon beginning a fellowship with the National Institute of Law Enforcement and Criminal Justice, I planned an audit of the status of this movement through an examination of current national legislation, and through an analysis of positions being taken by criminal justice and mental health professional organizations. For a variety of reasons this proved not to be a fruitful avenue of exploration, and I turned to the broader analysis reflected in this book.

Since the focus on current trends was retained, most of the material covers a relatively narrow slice of time. While it is thus less historical than some readers might prefer, the notes and references will lead the interested person to more of a long range perspective. It should be obvious that the problems and issues discussed here were a long time in developing and will not be easily resolved. In this context, I recognize that most, if not all, of the ideas and recommendations that follow have been discussed previously in one form or another. My goal has been to present evidence to indicate the need for continued concern over the development of the therapeutic state and the need to reconsider the issues. Earlier recognition of the problem has not resulted in most instances in significant policy changes, and the conventional wisdom of the movement seems to hold that the concern is exaggerated.

One additional word of explanation is necessary. Most of this book deals directly with relationships between the criminal justice and mental health systems, but there is some discussion of examples and behavior that do not violate criminal laws. This material is included because it reflects the general trend towards the medicalization of deviance, the role of the mental health system in the control of other forms of deviance, or issues relating to the role of the state in relation to its citizens.

Chapter 1

Introduction and Overview

Modern morality attributes behavior to circumstance; it thereby converts sin to sickness and erases fault. Its working hypothesis is that, if behavior is caused, its agent is not culpable.

Gwynn Nettler

It is an odd but perhaps accurate conclusion to note that the dependent and deviant may owe what freedom they have more to the fiscal conservatism of elected officials than to the benevolent motives of reformers.

David Rothman

LONDON (AP)—Nine young sailors from the crew of the U.S. nuclear submarine *Casimir Pulaski* are being sent home for medical care which the navy hopes will cure them of smoking marijuana. . . . The sailors were found in possession of marijuana and admitted using the drug. The navy exempts drug users from disciplinary proceedings if they agree to receive medical help.

The above news item, which appeared in newspapers in 1977, raises a number of interesting questions. Were these pot-smoking sailors committing a crime or exhibiting a sickness? They were being sent home for treatment, but would punishment of some sort have been a more rational response? Or, was being sent for treatment intended to be a punishment? Is it likely that the sailors thought of themselves as needing medical treatment? What kind of treatment does the physician offer when the sailor appears in his office? How does he know when to report back to the naval authorities that the sickness has been cured? If the sailors continue to smoke marijuana after having been treated, at what point does the problem stop being a sickness and become a sin? Or did everybody involved see this as a convenient solution to a situation that is not to be taken too seriously but that still calls for some kind of response?

This short account of the pot-smoking sailors serves as a parable for our times, for it reflects a number of current themes in our attempts to deal with troublesome behavior. Over the last ten to twenty years there has been a rapidly expanding tendency to define as sickness behavior that was earlier seen in moral terms. Many people previously considered to be in need of punishment—e.g., alcoholics, sex offenders, juvenile delinquents, drug abusers, shoplifters, child abusers, gamblers—are now seen as being in need of treatment. Increasingly, we have turned to medical experts to deal with all kinds of deviance, but we have grown to rely particularly heavily on mental health professionals. (It is a good bet that the medical help offered to the pot-smoking sailors came from a psychiatrist.) Just as the law replaced religion as the major social control system, the mental health system now encroaches on the legal system. Nicholas Kittrie, who has written about this subject in detail, predicts:

> For a long time to come both the system of criminal justice and the therapeutic state are likely to coexist as dual modes of social control. Increasingly, however, the therapeutic state will receive those offenders and deviants with whom society is willing to experiment through newer programs of rehabilitation and therapy. The therapeutic state is therefore likely to show the road toward more effective treatment techniques. Sometime, in an uncertain future, both modes are destined to merge into a unified system of social sanctions where individual guilt will be relatively irrelevant. . . .[1]

In elaborating on the concept of the therapeutic state, Kittrie points out that its foundation is "science," not faith, and that it feeds on the *parens patriae* power and the state responsibility for public welfare. However, it differs from the welfare state in that the latter makes its services available on a voluntary basis.

> Thus the need for social defense against those who exert little free will of their own, combined with the belief in scientific cure and with the state's traditional right and duty to exercise *parens patriae* functions, have

merged to form the new therapeutic state, which has assumed jurisdiction
to compel treatment of the unpunishables under the *parens patriae* power.[2]

Opinions differ as to how far we have come in terms of merging the
criminal justice and mental health systems. But there is no argument
that the two systems have increased their points of contact. We are a long
way from having reached the stage where individual guilt is considered
irrelevant, as the issue of responsibility continues to be a major source of
controversy. But what is evident is increased confusion regarding the
objectives of the two systems. Confusion and overlap in function is
apparent with respect to the goals of deterrence, incapacitation, retribu-
tion, and treatment. Although the social control functions of the mental
health system are now more openly recognized, we have not fully
appreciated the implications that come with this role.

In many respects, the increased contact between the two systems is a
rational and natural development. The types of people managed by the
criminal justice and mental health systems overlap considerably—they
come from the bottom of the socioeconomic scale and have limited social
skills, and minorities are overrepresented. In many instances, assignment to one category or the other is highly arbitrary, having more to do
with personal characteristics and administrative convenience than with
specific behavior or a meaningful classification system. Individuals are
frequently shifted back and forth from one institution to another—
prison, mental hospital, institution for the retarded, etc. (Recent research suggests that there is an inverse relationship between prison and
mental hospital populations—states with a higher prison population
tend to have a relatively low mental hospital population, and vice
versa.[3]) The forensic units in state mental hospitals have steadily grown,
and as the census in mental hospitals has decreased, prisoners have been
moved into the vacant buildings. This commonality of interest and
function has not been restricted to the institutional level. Federally
funded community mental health centers are now required to provide
services to the criminal justice system at the local level, and the use of
mental health professionals in the early stages of the processing of
offenders has increased dramatically. To understand these recent events,
we need to look at development within the two systems over the last
twenty to twenty-five years.

THE CURRENT STATUS OF THE CRIMINAL JUSTICE AND MENTAL HEALTH SYSTEMS

The mental health field can reasonably be described as a rapid
growth industry. The movement was relatively nonexistent before the

Second World War. Yet it is currently estimated that in the United States $17 billion are spent annually in providing direct mental health care; indirect costs total an additional $20 billion.[4] Given the well-known tendency of professional groups to expand the number and kinds of people needing their services, it is not surprising that one of the first acts of the 1977 President's Commission on Mental Health was to increase by 50 percent the number of people judged to have mental problems. The commission reported that new evidence reveals that 15 percent of the American population, amounting to between 20 and 32 million people, need some form of mental health care at any one time. Even these figures do not take into account the special needs of school-age children (an estimated 15 percent of whom need help with psychological disorders), 500,000 Americans who are dependent on heroin, 10 million people with significant and recent alcohol-related problems, the elderly, etc.[5]

The decisionmaking power that has been assigned to mental health professionals goes far beyond what anyone would have predicted even a few years ago. They contribute to decisions about child custody, divorce, abortion, sterilization, presentence reports, jury selection, classification of prisoners, the management of terrorists, competency to stand trial, commitment to hospitals, and almost any other issue of significance on the current scene.

Jonas Robitscher, a psychiatrist who recently received the Isaac Ray Award from the American Psychiatric Association, may have overstated things when he said that psychiatrists hold more power than any other contemporary figures, but he may not have been off the mark when he referred to much of this power as unobserved and unchecked.

> To detail all of the abuses of psychiatry would take a book . . . but the most interesting aspect of all this to my mind is that while all these psychiatric injustices were being demonstrated, psychiatry continued to wax strong and to grow. The tremendous authority that psychiatrists have gathered has not appreciably been reduced by legal and other professional and journalistic attacks on how psychiatrists use their power. In fact, the community health movement and the concept of the right to mental health treatment have increased the importance of the psychiatrist in our society.[6]

The growth of the mental health system was paralleled by a similar expansion of activity within the criminal justice system. Public expenditures for criminal justice reached almost $20 billion by 1976, and the system employed over a million people full time.[7] By the end of 1978, a record 307,384 persons were held under the jurisdiction of federal and state correctional authorities (a 3-percent increase over the previous year),[8] with another 140,000 locked in local jails and almost 50,000 youths in state and local facilities.[9] Approximately 2 million people are locked up or are under official supervision on any given day, and this does not include the increasing number of family members encouraged or required to accept treatment when one of them is in trouble with the law.[10] By the mid-1970s, court dockets were jammed and state prisons were being temporarily closed because of overcrowding. In spite of a growing recognition that imprisonment often does more harm than good, the states continued to imprison at the highest rate in the world and to pass out the harshest sentences in the Western world.[11]

Given these circumstances, it is not hard to see why the criminal justice system might be eager to transfer some of its load. It was a natural thing to fall in with the general cultural trend to turn to the mental health professionals for help with all kinds of problems. Even though the two systems may not have been ready for a merger, they were at least ready for a fair amount of contact. Not that each didn't hold reservations about the other: people within the mental health system tended to think of criminal justice as brutal and harmful, while people within the criminal justice system were skeptical about the mental health professionals' motives and effectiveness.

The increased contact between the two systems came at a time when both were undergoing significant change. Serious questions have been raised for the mental health field about the appropriateness of the medical model, the effectiveness of treatment, and the unreliability of classification. Concern about the use of coercion has mounted, and mental patient rights groups and public interest law groups concerned with mental health have developed rapidly. Thomas Szasz is no longer alone as a critic of the mental health system, as the attack was joined in 1978 by the authors of titles such as *The Mind Stealers, Mind Control, The Psychological Society,* and *The Machine That Oils Itself.*[12] During the early seventies, the courts handed down a number of decisions relating to civil commitment, the right to treatment, due process procedures, etc. All of this furthered the deinstitutionalization movement that started in 1955. But twenty years later, a strong backlash had developed in response to what was perceived as the "dumping" of mental patients in the community, as local police complained that their jails were filling up with former patients who should not have been released from the hospital.

Thinking about the criminal justice system was also undergoing change. For approximately a hundred years the correctional system had functioned on the premise that its major purpose was rehabilitation. By the late 1960s and early 1970s, it was clear to everyone that this objective had never been attained. A dominant theme of the time was expressed by Norman Carlson, director of the Justice Department's Bureau of Prisons:

> "The concept of rehabilitation fits not only our religious beliefs about the perfectability of mankind, but also our utilitarian desire to reduce the impact of crime by preventing crime at the source . . . The vast majority of offenders have no serious mental disease or defect. Crime may be a plague on society, but it is not a disease for which we have a guaranteed cure."[13]

Carlson went on to say that the abandonment of the rehabilitation ideology and its attendant notions of professional intervention did not imply a reactionary abandonment of the inmates themselves, but only the relinquishment of the "medical model" and coerced treatment. He was expressing a position being taken by a number of people who were pushing for the elimination of discretion in sentencing, a concern with "just deserts" and a focus on incapacitation and deterrence as opposed to treatment of offenders. In contrast to the practice of the last hundred years, the new focus was to be upon the "act" and not the "actor." The following kind of statement was typical:

> "To sum up, I both favor and predict a criminal law which is openly and sincerely penal in outlook and does not try to take refuge behind benevolent rhetoric about treating and rehabilitating deviants; a criminal law, that is, based primarily on general deterrence and considerations of justice."[14]

These objectives were elaborated in a series of books that were in some instances written by people who otherwise held widely different perspectives on the causes and management of crime.[15]

Support for the above movement was found in social scientists' repeated documentation that nothing seemed to work. Some experts seemed to take a perverse kind of pleasure from an "evaluation of evaluations" that reviewed several hundred studies and concluded that efforts at rehabilitation were useless.[16]

Thus we have entered a period of considerable confusion regarding the appropriate public policy towards the management of troublesome people. In such a period, the predominant ideology takes on special significance. We turn now to a brief examination of ideology as background for much of the discussion to follow.

IDEOLOGY AND POLICY

Walter Miller has provided a helpful framework for this discussion.[17] He defines ideology as a set of general and abstract beliefs or assumptions about the correct or proper state of things, particularly with respect to the moral order and political arrangements that serve to shape one's positions on specific issues. Miller suggests that beliefs about criminal justice can be placed on a scale with a zero midpoint and left and right polar positions, and then he outlines the major general assumptions associated with the polar positions. These points are developed in some detail, but the outline in Table 1 conveys the central ideas. Although Miller's discussion relates to criminal justice, most of his points are equally applicable to general deviance and the mental health system.

This outline highlights two basic themes that dominate much of the discussion in this book—the rights of the individual versus society (from the family on up), and the role of free will or choice in human behavior. These are central issues that cut across a number of policy decisions, and few would pretend that solutions to them are out there simply waiting to be discovered.

This is not the place to attempt to summarize (if, indeed, that were possible) the continuing debate on individual responsibility, or that on collective versus individual rights. But it is exactly on these points that professional journals are filled, court decisions are passed down (though not necessarily obeyed), and laws passed. For example, in spite of court and legislative decisions defining alcoholism and drug addition as diseases, we still have not decided how we feel about these problems. ("At some point in the process, the alcoholic made the decision to take the first drink.") And we are equally ambivalent about a number of other questions. Does not the family of the mentally ill person have some rights that justify civil commitment, regardless of other concerns? Is the criminal justice system primarily concerned with the law as an external constraint (law and order), or as an agency fostering the internalization of control (social justice)? How much of the blame should be assigned to the individual and how much to society? Is crime primarily a managerial problem rather than a reflection of social malaise? And so on.

At an abstract level, many people have no difficulty deciding where they would fall on Miller's scale. But when we turn to the day-to-day operations of the criminal justice and mental health systems, the situation is not all that clear. In the first place, questions about responsibility and individual liberty are not constantly under review by

Table 1. Ideology and Criminal Justice

LEFT										RIGHT
5	4	3	2	1	0	1	2	3	4	5

Paramount Value: JUSTICE
General Assumptions

1. Primary responsibility for criminal behavior lies in society and social conditions.

2. The social control system is deficient, based on obsolete morality geared to sustain special interest groups.

3. Power is distributed inequitably and unjustly.

4. The official system makes distinctions based on major categories or classes—e.g., age, sex, race, criminal–noncriminal.

5. The system creates more deviance than it cures.

6. The total range of behavior under criminal sanctions is excessively broad.

Crusading Issues on the Left

1. Overcriminalization.
2. Labeling and stigmatization.
3. Overinstitutionalization.
4. Overcentralization.
5. Discriminatory bias.

Paramount Value: ORDER
General Assumptions

1. The individual is responsible for his or her behavior.

2. We must have a strong moral order.

3. There is a need to secure the major areas of customary activity (safety from crime on the streets, etc.).

4. Legitimate authority must be adhered to.

5. Human relations are ordered on the basis of distinctions among major categories of persons (age, sex, etc.).

Crusading Issues on the Right

1. Excessive leniency towards lawbreakers.
2. The favoring of the welfare and rights of lawbreakers over victims.
3. The erosion of discipline and respect for constituted authority.
4. The cost of crime.
5. Excessive permissiveness.

Source: Adapted from W. G. Miller, "Ideology and criminal justice policy: some current issues, *Journal of Criminal Law and Criminology*, 1973, 64, 141–162.

most people; they are not considered and dismissed as irrelevant or already decided, but are more likely not to be considered at all. The primary concerns of people on the job usually relate to personal and professional objectives of keeping the machinery of the organization moving, solving the day's tasks, and satisfying mutual needs. Polar positions are moderated into shades of gray, if considered at all. In addition, very few people accept in pure form the basic assumptions of the two systems—that a person is free to choose to do or not to do what the laws require (criminal justice), or that a person is solely a product of environment or the helpless victim of a disease (mental health).

Adjustments are made, so that even when people's beliefs start out at widely differing points ideologically, actions tend not to be so disparate in practice. For example, "just deserts" and determinate sentencing proposals have brought together some interesting combinations of people with very different hopes for the movement. Some want merely to limit discretion, while others hope to lock up a larger number of people for a longer period of time.

The role of ideology has been illustrated interestingly by the response to a recent report from St. Elizabeths Hospital in Washington, D.C. Samuel Yochelson, a psychiatrist, and Stanton Samenow, a psychologist, published the results of years of study of mentally ill offenders under the title *The Criminal Personality*.[18] The essential finding of this work is the discovery of a criminal personality, evident early in life, not believed to be caused by psychological or sociological deprivation. The authors conclude that criminals can be identified by their personality characteristics and particularly by fifty-two "errors of thinking" that set them apart. They find no difference between criminals who were designated mentally ill and those who were not; that criminals are very much in control of themselves; and that the criminal insanity plea is a charade engaged in equally by the courts, the criminals, and society. Career criminals are seen as committing crimes by free choice, and are believed to be capable of reform if they choose to alter radically their thinking process (with the expectation that most will not). Change is brought about by an "unashamedly moral approach" that emphasizes "guilt rather than forgiveness." We need not be concerned at this point about the merits of the work, but focus instead on the response to it, for indeed, the work has received considerable attention—national coverage on television, numerous newspaper stories, editorials, and requests for Samenow to speak (Yochelson is now dead).

The ideological dimensions are apparent in the source of this attention. To the seeming dismay of Samenow, they consistently come from the right side of Miller's scale. And the support is almost always couched alongside pejorative words and phrases such as: "It is time to end permissive, coddling measures"; "This will make the Freudians, liberals, and bleeding hearts scream out loud"; "This will take away the 'look what society made of me' crutch." The commentators frequently go on to state that the work merits more attention than it will receive, and express concern that attempts will be made to block the book. Pleas are made for immediate paperback editions and widespread dissemination. Praise comes from *U.S. Medicine, The Catholic Worker,* and conservative columnist Max Rafferty. Requests for speeches come almost exclusively from departments of corrections and prosecutors, with silence from the other half of the ideological scale (except for negative reviews in professional journals). In many instances it is apparent that the editorial writers have not read the book, but are responding to their affinity for what they take to be the central message.

Even some of those with serious reservations end up deferring to the credentials of the authors—e.g., "And, finally, it is a matter of no small importance that the Program for the Investigation of Criminal Behavior is an official U.S. Government project providing resources that only a great government can supply."[19] The reviewer who wrote this must have had a very limited contact indeed with government supported projects, and with the basis of authority for researchers working in this area.

It is interesting to note that those outside the field of corrections have been critical of the work on scientific grounds. (My own reading of the work is that it is purely clinical, highly subjective, and without empirical value). Whatever the ultimate worth of the ideas presented, the research that the authors describe cannot be said to corroborate their conclusions. But the important point to be made here concerns the public's response. Crime is widely recognized as the major concern of many people who are pessimistic about the probability of reform and who like the idea of individuals being held responsible for their behavior. The counseling program offered in *The Criminal Personality* has considerable appeal for these people: the criminal is told he will get no sympathy; that he, alone, is responsible for his problems; that he and his crimes are contemptible; and that sociological and psychological jargon will not be accepted as excuses for bad behavior. This perspective evokes an immediate supportive response that is not related in any way to the substance of the work.

It is this response to *The Criminal Personality* that many mental health professionals find very hard to accept—that is, the ideological themes far outweigh the substantive base of a given work. Many have even argued that social science research in general tends to follow, rather than precede, public policy decisions. Henry Aaron comes to this conclusion after reviewing the role of the federal government in its capacity to bring about change in three areas—poverty and discrimination, education and training, and unemployment and inflation:

> . . . the parallel between development of social science and the views of scholars, on the one hand, and developments of public policy during this period, on the other, was striking in each of these three areas. But in many cases, the findings of social science seemed to come after, rather than before, change in policy, which suggests that political events may influence scholars more than research influences policy.[20]

Aaron goes on to suggest that the social science contribution is usually not so much specific information and conclusions as it is a contribution to a general perspective. Much of the research within social science turns out to be flawed, criticized, and rejected. Repeatedly, the function of social science seems to be that of searching out weaknesses and uncovering the failures of programs. Given this, policymakers are prone to ignore research findings when they conflict with deeply held beliefs and predetermined positions. This is particularly true in the emotionally charged areas that are the subject of this book, and should be kept in mind for all of the discussion that follows.

We need to note that relationships between ideology and practice frequently fail to be consistent and immutable. For example, we are currently entering a period of renewed interest in the organic, genetic, and biochemical causes of crime. It has been my experience that many of those who hold such theories simultaneously favor strong sanctions against offenders. That is, we end up with the peculiar situation in which punishment is deemed to be appropriate for groups of people who presumably are not responsible for their behavior. If we do find that troublesome behavior has its roots in organic conditions, where does that leave us in terms of punishment? Do we decide then that we have a surplus population, somehow different and less human than the rest of us, and therefore appropriately subject to banishment or annihilation?[21] Or, as some of the behaviorists suggest, can we put aside questions of moral responsibility and simply focus on modifying the undesirable behavior?

Finally, it is important to acknowledge that even the most firmly held beliefs tend to disappear under the pressure of economic forces. Illustrations of this fact can be found ín a number of very different contexts. A conservative San Diego grand jury, upon discovering the relationship between crime and addiction within its community, recommends making drugs freely available to addicts. Mental hospitals and institutions for juveniles are kept open because of their economic impact on the community rather than policy reasons relating to treatment. Release rates from prisons are directly related to the number of new prisoners awaiting admission.[22] Supreme Court decisions are simply ignored when the costs are judged to be too high (e.g., a recent national study of the Argersinger case, requiring the provision of a lawyer for any defendant facing the possibility of jail, has been essentially ignored.[23] Those who oppose ideologically the construction of additional prisons have learned to present their arguments in economic terms, as these are the only factors that seem to carry much weight. Decisions to prosecute, incarcerate, or divert individuals from the criminal justice system are most heavily shaped by the processing capacity of the various elements of the system. Regardless of the best intentions, major policies are frequently determined by the economic environment. For example, those who would advocate programs of primary prevention in mental health are stymied by the large role played by insurance programs that reimburse only remedial services. In short, spirited debate is strong in the areas discussed herein, but it is consistently overshadowed by the mandates of day-to-day operations and economic concerns.

OVERVIEW

A number of people would argue that concern over the therapeutic state is dated and misplaced. Evidence that would support this view would appear to be abundant—the "just deserts" movement, the extension of due process protections to an ever increasing number of people and situations, recent court decisions, tightened commitment laws, deinsitutionalization, the growth of advocacy programs, the right to refuse treatment, etc. All of this has led to a strong feeling that we have backed away from the coercive use of the mental health system in the management of deviance. My position is that such a view represents a serious misreading of the evidence, and that the movement is continuing to gather steam. Although corrective steps have been taken to deal with the most flagrant abuses of discretion in the name of treatment, I contend that there are large gaps in implementation, and that in many instances the discretion has been shifted to earlier and less visible points in the system. The denial that there is a problem and the current national mood calling for a "get tough" response to all kinds of deviance should be signals of concern in and of themselves.

Certainly there are benefits to be derived from increased contact between the criminal justice and mental health systems. But these need to be specifically identified and weighed against the losses. There is no easy solution to the problems discussed in this book, but a recognition of them might lead to fairer management in the short run, with desirable consequences for the functioning of both systems of control.

In the discussion that follows, references to the criminal justice system are meant to include the entire spectrum from the police to the prisons. References to the mental health system are equally comprehensive and refer to private practitioners, community mental health centers, and mental hospitals. The boundaries of the mental health system are extremely amorphous, and could be taken to encompass most human service agencies. There is also considerable role confusion and overlap of function among the traditional mental health professionals. Thus in many instances when a reference is made to psychiatry, the reader can appropriately substitute "mental health professional."

The concepts of rehabilitation and treatment are also used in a very broad sense. This can lead to some problems—for example, in a given instance "treatment" might refer to a very specific activity, such as the administration of a drug or of a unique form of psychotherapy—while in another instance the reference might be to something as vague as the "recreational therapy" of allowing a patient to attend a movie or take a walk. Rehabilitation might include all of the above plus a wide range of educational and social services. My defense for the use of these terms in this general manner is the belief that it reflects reality, that programs and services are usually delivered in this general manner.

The focus in the analysis that follows is almost exclusively on adults. Many of the conclusions that are drawn could apply equally as well to the managment of troublesome children, but such an analysis creates special problems that are best considered separately.

The next chapter provides an update on a number of behaviors that have been designated sicknesses, rather than sins, and documentation of the current trend towards the medicalization of deviance.[24] Chapter 3 contains a detailed review of current court decisions as they relate in one way or another to the therapeutic state. This is followed in Chapter 4 by an outline of the forces bringing the criminal justice and mental health systems into amalgamation. The problems that accompany this merger are then reviewed in Chapter 5, followed in Chapter 6 by specific recommendations to deal with these problems.

NOTES

1. Kittrie, N. N. *The Right to be Different: Deviance and Enforced Therapy.* Johns Hopkins Press, 1971, p. 407.
2. Ibid., p. 41.
3. Brenner, H. Seminar presented at National Institute of Law Enforcement and Criminal Justice, November 1977.

4. President's Commission on Mental Health. Vol. I, U.S. Government Printing Office, 1978, p. 4.
5. Ibid., pp. 8–9.
6. Robitscher, J. Isaac Ray lectures delivered at George Washington University, November 1977. Also, see *Journal of Psychiatry & Law,* 1977, 5, 603–624.
7. Expenditure and Employment Data for the Criminal Justice System, 1976, Advanced Report. U.S. Department of Commerce, Bureau of the Census. U.S. Department of Justice, National Criminal Justice Information and Statistics Service. January 1978.
8. Prisoners in State and Federal Institutions, December 31, 1978. U.S. Department of Justice, National Criminal Justice Information and Statistics Service, National Prisoner Statistics Bulletin SD-NPS-PSF-6A, May 1979.
9. Brodsky, S. L. Ethical issues for psychologists in corrections. Workshop on corrections, Task Force on the Role of Psychology in the Criminal Justice System, American Psychological Association (Washington, D.C., September 8–9, 1977).
10. Messinger, S. L. Punishments' troubling future. *Chicago Tribune,* December 16, 1977.
11. Doleschal, E. Rate and length of imprisonment. *Crime & Delinquency,* 1977, 23, 51–56.
12. Chavkin, S., *The Mind Stealers,* Houghton Mifflin, 1978; Schrag, P., *Mind Control,* Pantheon, 1978; Gross, M. L., *The Psychological Society,* Random House, 1978; Reinehr, R. C., *The Machine That Oils Itself: A Critical Look at the Mental Health Establishment,* Nelson-Hall, 1975.
13. Testimony before U.S. Senate Subcommittee, quoted in *Behavior Today,* 1977, 8, No. 42, October 31.
14. Andenaes, J. *Punishment and Deterrence.* University of Michigan Press, 1974, p. 168.
15. American Friends Service Committee, *Struggle for Justice,* Hill & Wang, 1971; Wilson, J. Q., *Thinking About Crime,* Basic Books, 1975; Neier, A., *Crime and Punishment,* Stein and Day, 1976; Van Den Haag, E., *Punishing Criminals,* Basic Books, 1975; Von Hirsch, A., *Doing Justice,* Hill & Wang, 1976.
16. Lipton, D., Martinson, R., and Wilks, J. *The Effectiveness of Correctional Treatment: A Survey of Treatment Evaluation.* Praeger, 1975.
17. Miller, W. B. Ideology and criminal justice policy: some current issues. *Journal of Criminal Law and Criminology,* 1973, 64, 141–162.
18. Yochelson, S., and Samenow, S. E. *The Criminal Personality,* Vol. I, *A Profile for Change,* Jason Aronson, 1976; Vol. II, *The Change Process,* Jason Aronson, 1977.
19. Borken, J. Review of S. Yochelson and S. E. Samenow, *The Criminal Personality,* in *Federal Bar Journal,* 1976, 35, p. 241.
20. Aaron, H. J. *Politics and the Professors.* The Brookings Institution, 1978, p. 9.
21. For a discussion of this point, see Rubinstein, R., *The Cunning of History,* Harper & Row, 1975.
22. Eck, J. An aggregate population dynamics model of the Michigan prison system. University of Michigan, 1977. Mimeo.
23. Krantz, S., Smith, C., Rossman, D., Froyd, P., and Hoffman, J. *Right to Counsel in Criminal Cases: The Mandate of Argersinger v. Hamlin.* Ballinger, 1976.
24. For a general discussion of the medicalization of deviance, see: Conrad, P., The discovery of hyperkinesia: notes on the medicalization of deviant behavior, *Social Problems,* 1977, 23, 12–21; Zola, I. K., Medicine as an institution of social control, *Sociological Review,* 1972, 20, 487–504.

Chapter 2

Examples of the Transfer from Criminal Justice to Mental Health

Theoretically, attempts to reduce "right" or "wrong" to "healthy" or "unhealthy" merely disguise and shift moral problems from one forum to another without solving them.

Ernest van den Haag

When poverty, or racism, or crime, is labeled a health problem, then society can defer to experts for its solution, and everyone else is free to go on with business as usual.

Judge David Bazelon

We now turn to an examination of law violations that are specifically defined as diseases rather than crimes and are thus subject to treatment instead of punishment. Some of the topics to be discussed have been reviewed in detail by other writers, and need not be developed extensively here. My purpose here is to assess specific examples of the mental health system's involvement in matters that were formerly considered to come under the jurisdiction of criminal justice. In every instance some interplay continues between the two systems, with the balance shifting somewhat for each of the problem behaviors under consideration. My basic thesis is that the overall trend is an expansion of the number and kinds of behaviors considered to be sicknesses and thus subject to control by the mental health system.

PUBLIC DRUNKENNESS

The most complete transfer of a large class of individuals from the criminal justice system to the health care system is probably best illustrated by alcoholism.

As of December 1976, twenty-three states, the District of Columbia, and Puerto Rico had enacted a uniform alcoholism act that includes decriminalization of public drunkenness. Eleven other states have enacted some form of legislation that achieved essentially the same purpose.[1] The impetus for this movement came in part from special federal grants earmarked specifically for states that have decriminalized public drunkenness. Public inebriates in these states are not to be arrested but ignored, taken home, or delivered to a detoxification center. What is particularly striking is that this transformation in policy has become relatively complete within a very short period of time. Not until 1951 (a date that parallels the rapid development of the mental health movement) did the World Health Organization define alcoholism as a disease, and it was only in 1970 that the National Institute on Alcohol Abuse and Alcoholism was established within the Department of Health, Education, and Welfare.

The movement to define alcoholism as a disease has been endorsed by all the major medical organizations, and even by the American Bar Association. Currently there is a strong but controversial effort to increase and broaden health insurance coverage for alcohol treatment throughout the United States. The success of this attempt will be moderated in part by budgetary constraints, and in part by lingering objections to paying for benefits to treat a condition that some still consider to be self-inflicted.

The growing support for defining alcohol abuse as a disease is further indicated by the Law Enforcement Assistance Administration (LEAA)'s spending roughly $10 million on the problem in fiscal 1974, "from the criminal justice point of view," with the major portion going for treatment.[2] Nationally there has been a dramatic decrease in arrests for drunkenness and disorderly conduct, even in those states that have not yet passed decriminalization acts.[3]

An Attorney General's opinion on the Rehabilitation Act of 1973 permits the designation of alcoholics and drug addicts as "handicapped," with the interpretation that it is unlawful for employers to discriminate against individuals simply because of alcohol or drug addiction.[4] Another federal law prohibits discrimination in outpatient clinics and hospitals.[5]

As a means of insuring that at least certain alcoholics receive treatment, Congress amended the Social Security Act in 1975 to require any person disabled by drug addiction or alcoholism to undergo treatment in order to receive benefits. Furthermore, supplemental security income benefits must be paid to a person or agency interested in the individual's welfare rather than to the individual himself or herself (presumably to prevent the individual from using the money to buy alcohol).[6]

However, not everyone subscribes to the theory that public drunkenness should go unpunished. It was still necessary in 1977 for a judge to rule that "it is an unconstitutional imposition of cruel and unusual punishment to jail and convict a person who can successfully plead he suffers from alcoholism to the point where he cannot take care of himself and cannot refrain from drinking in public."[7] The judge commented that the criminal process assumes that the only way to help an alcoholic is to "dry him out," but that frequently due process rights are ignored. As an example of this he cites a jurisdiction in California, where there were 1,319 not-guilty pleas in 1975, but only three trials. More than a third of the defendants served an average of twenty-five days in jail awaiting trial. Typically, the case either was dropped at the time of trial or the defendant pleaded guilty and was given a sentence of the "time already served." Thus for all practical purposes the defendant received punishment before trial, making the trial irrelevant.

DRUG ABUSE

When an agency responsible for controlling a particular form of deviance tells us how big the problem is, it is usually safe to assume that the figures are inflated. It is indeed rare for an organization to underestimate the number of people deemed to need its services. (On the other hand, the prevalence of transient deviance of all kinds within the general population is much higher than most of us suspect.) As the federal organizations to fight drugs grew under President Nixon, so did the estimated number of addicts. In 1968, the official figure for the nation's entire addict population was 63,000. By the end of 1972, only four years later, the figure officially promulgated as the number of persons addicted to drugs in the United States had reached 600,000.[8] The head of the national drug program was quoted in the fall of 1977 as saying that a million people in the United States had tried heroin; 247,000 were in treatment programs, and another two or three hundred thousand addicts were on the streets.[9] In the face of this growth there has been considerable debate as to whether these people are bad or sick, and whether they should be imprisoned or treated (or both).

There is considerable reason to believe that the sickness perspective is prevailing. As indicated above, treatment programs have expanded rapidly, and diversion programs now exist in all major urban areas. Federally funded diversion programs such as TASC (Treatment Alternatives to Street Crime) have consistently been successful in obtaining state and local support at the end of the federal funding period,[10] and some evidence exists that professionals at all points in the criminal justice system strongly support diversion programs for drug abusers.[11] Further backing for treatment was found in a recent survey in which 61 percent of all prison inmates reported a history of illicit drug use, of whom less than 15 percent had received any treatment. Thus in December 1977, LEAA announced the commitment of one million dollars for pilot programs in four states. The proposed programs call for six to nine months of therapy, then early release, followed by nine months of treatment in community-based drug programs.[12]

It is interesting to note that, just as with alcoholism, the government is seeking insurance coverage for drug treatment. It has recently underwritten a $167,000 study of whether private health insurance plans should provide prepaid benefits for full treatment of drug abusers. Most of the sixty-nine Blue Cross plans currently provide some coverage for drug abuse, but it is usually limited to paying for hospitalization of drug abusers who suffer physical or mental complications.

As with other problem behaviors discussed in this chapter, it is not always easy to discern the basis of support for the management of drug abuse as a sickness. Some of it certainly must stem from the view that drug abuse is a disease beyond the control of the individual, and is thus a medical problem calling for treatment instead of punishment. Other support undoubtedly comes from the pressure on the part of the criminal justice system to find any alternative which would reduce the caseload, regardless of particular perspectives on the nature of drug abuse. And finally, some of the support for diversion must come out of a feeling that in fact some "treatment" is punishment. The popularity of TASC programs must be due in part to the direct social control role that they and many drug treatment programs play . The monitoring of clients and prompt reporting of violations to courts is seen as one of the most important features of the program.[13]

The Drug Use/Misuse Panel of the President's Commission on Mental Health describes the goals of drug treatment as inextricably intertwined with those of law enforcement.[14] According to its report, the expansion of the drug treatment system stemmed directly from concern about the relationship between drug abuse and crime, with the goal of getting the deviants off the streets. The criminal justice system thus became the major case finding mechanism and the treatment staff became the moral equivalent of parole officers.

> Diversion from the criminal justice system can take many forms. Offenders can be diverted before booking, before trial, at the time of sentencing, as a condition of probation or parole, and so on; the treatment system is virtually obligated to accept all such diversions in order to maintain their funding. In fact, many treatment programs not only are willing to accept such clients, but have set up liaisons with the courts and police, and have become an active part of the diversion process. The treatment programs have lost control to their main funding source, and consequently, the efficacy and integrity of the services which they can provide are in serious jeopardy. [15]

The drug use/misuse task force goes on to argue that collusion between the two systems has been so insidious that the goals of each have been distorted, and the treatment system has become less and less distant from the criminal justice system.

It is interesting to note that the two problem areas most closely associated with crime—alcohol and drug abuse—are the two areas most subject to medicalization and diversion from the criminal justice system.

SEXUAL DEVIANCE

It was within the realm of sex that we used to know most clearly what was acceptable and what was unacceptable, and who was to be punished in what way when they violated the norms. Today, however, we're not sure which laws to ignore, change, or enforce. Since Kinsey, we have been confused about sexual "normality," and behavior forbidden in the recent past is now an accepted part of therapy—e.g., masturbation and the use of prostitutes as therapists. Given this state of affairs, it is no wonder that we have sought some new experts to help us—and again have found the mental health professionals ready to offer assistance.

The current debate over homosexuality is informative. It was less than twenty years ago that the Florida legislature established a special committee whose main function was to ferret out homosexuals, run them through the courts, publish their names by the hundreds in newspapers, and eventually send a few of them on to "treatment." (The committee suffered some embarrassment when an unwitting aide had its report published with a purple cover showing two nude men embracing, insuring an immediate high demand for the report for the wrong reasons.) There was some question about the normality of everybody involved with the committee, but for those who were arrested for homosexuality there was a formal diagnostic label in the manual of the American Psychiatric Association. This label was removed from the list of official disorders in 1973 by the board of trustees of the association, a move later supported by a poll of the membership. A majority of those responding in a more recent poll have again deemed homosexuality a disorder—a "pathological adaptation." And a committee has now proposed a new category—"ego-dystonic homosexuality"—that includes homosexuality involving emotional distress.[16] A number of additional interesting details surround these events, but this outline suffices for our purposes.

The question of whether homosexuality is an illness is important because it has implications for other rights and other areas of behavior. Several things should be noted. First, it is significant that such a "scientific" decision should be made by majority vote—and a closely divided one. A quote from Dr. Henry Brill, chairman of a task force that considered the issue, is informative: "To be blunt about it, with the present state of our knowledge . . . there's no way of measuring an illness or its absence. Professionals depend upon a sort of consensus that is subject to change under different social conditions."[17] Secondly, the details surrounding both votes revealed that it was a highly political action. The results of the second vote may simply reflect the current reaction to the gay rights movement and psychiatry's desire to retain responsibility for dealing with the problem.

The attempt to remove homosexuality from both the sickness and sin categories has had very limited success, and for a good while to come both definitions are likely to prevail to some extent. The situation in Florida, for example, has not changed much since the legislative committee hunted homosexuals; police still patrol the public men's rooms in Tallahassee, as they do in major cities across the country. No one is immune to arrest, including U.S. congressmen and others of comparable status. Once an arrest has been made (at least for individuals such as those just cited), the courts seem willing to accept a sickness definition. From the available evidence, the person usually enters psychiatric treatment, and charges are subsequently dismissed.

Recent court decisions are relevant to the sin-sickness controversy regarding homosexuality. The admissions committee of the Florida bar, unable to decide the appropriateness of admitting applicants who acknowledged a homosexual preference, asked for a ruling from the state supreme court. The court stated that the *expression* of such preferences did not preclude admission to the bar, but reserved the possibility that *acting* upon the preference might do so.[18] The constitutionality of state laws making it a crime for consenting adults to engage in homosexual acts in private was upheld by a 1978 U.S. Supreme Court decision.[19] The particular case before the Court involved blatant entrapment of Eugene E., a resident of Jacksonville, North Carolina. Mr. E., the operator of an adult bookstore and massage parlor, had openly acknowledged his homosexuality. In order to "run him out of town," a detective hired a seventeen-year-old Marine to complete a sex act with Mr. E. in the privacy of the latter's home. Subsequently Mr. E. was arrested and sentenced to a year in jail.[20]

There is an important distinction between the case of Mr. E., an avowed gay, and cases such as the congressman mentioned above. The latter define their behavior in terms of sickness, stress, depression, etc., and acknowledge the need for professional help. Mr. E. did not consider himself sick or depressed (and at the same time was undoubtedly being punished for his association with the adult bookstore and massage parlor).

Two other recent court cases involve individuals who openly acknowledged their gayness. In one of these, a teacher's support of gay rights was interpreted by two psychiatrists as deviation from normal mental health; in view of this finding, the board of education's requirement that the teacher undergo a psychiatric exam was found to be fair and reasonable.[21] In a similar situation in the state of Washington, the school board was more straightforward in firing an avowed homosexual because his sexual preference constituted immorality.[22] In these and similar situations, it is reasonable to assume that some of the community response stems from objections to the public profession of gayness, and to the denial that it is wrong or sick. Gays' aggressive demand for rights is probably directly related to the recent repeal of antidiscrimination clauses on the grounds of sexual preference in Dade County, Florida, St. Paul, Minnesota, and Wichita, Kansas.

The illness model has been applied to other forms of sexual behavior that were formerly considered moral in nature, as shown in the following three examples. In 1970, a San Francisco woman was awarded $50,000 for the disease of nymphomania, which was said to have been caused by a cable car accident. She admitted to having had over a hundred lovers following the accident and having engaged in sexual intercourse fifty times in five days. Four psychiatrists and seven other medical experts testified in her behalf.[23] This case can be understood only as an extreme example of the willingness of the public (as represented by the jury) to place its faith in science and the medical expert—in a situation that would normally evoke skepticism and extreme doubt.

A further illustration of faith in the medical expert can be found in the 1975 Georgia Statutes. In Georgia, a person charged with the possession of obscene material now has an affirmative defense when the receipt of such material was authorized in writing by a licensed physician or psychiatrist. Thus the family physician has the authority to sanction the reading of dirty books.

Another interesting example of the medicalization of sexual behavior can be found in a bill introduced in the Florida House of Representatives —The Prostitution and Rehabilitation Act of 1977.[24] This act provided for the decriminalization of prostitution and required the Mental Health Program Office of the Department of Health and Rehabilitative Services to formulate and effect a plan for the rehabilitation and treatment of prostitutes, and to promulgate health standards to protect the public from ongoing prostitution. The law, of course, provided for a fee system based upon the prostitute's ability to pay (which is consistent with the general practice of involuntarily hospitalizing people for mental illness and then charging them for treatment that they have not requested). Nationally, organizations of prostitutes have resisted moves to apply the pathology label to prostitution and have indicated that they have no need or desire for "treatment" provided by the state.

Over thirty states have special laws dealing with sex offenders. The aim of these special statutes is to provide treatment for individuals who are thought to be dangerous and mentally ill, and to simultaneously protect the public. These statutes have come under attack because of vagueness, inadequate due process of law, the absence of treatment in the institutions to which the offenders are committed, and a failure to achieve the avowed purposes.[25] Apparently in many instances the most dangerous men are rejected under the laws because they are not amenable to treatment, while the least dangerous are retained. We have here another major category in which the mental health system is deemed the appropriate one to exercise social control, a viewpoint that has prevailed in the face of heavy criticism.

GAMBLING

Compulsive gambling is a progressive behavior disorder that we psychiatrists must look on as we do any other very serious emotional illness. Unfortunately, one of the things I hear from a few of the psychiatrists I talk to about this is that they feel that the compulsive gambler is someone who could control his gambling on his own if he really wanted to. Well, I would hope that psychiatrists who think this way, or who have the feeling that somehow these are "bad" people, don't ever attempt to treat them. They're doomed to failure right from the start. But if you do recognize compulsive gambling as an illness, you can be of tremendous help. And this work is too rich in psychological material. Gamblers' fantasies, their magical thinking, rationalizations, denials, their almost delusional type of optimism, are fascinating.[26]

The statement above is that of Robert L. Custer, of the Veterans Administration headquarters in Washington, D.C. It summarizes one current perspective on gambling that defines it as a disease similar to alcoholism. Its victims are said to have many of the same personality defects as alcoholics and to be in need of treatment similar to that provided alcoholics. It is estimated that at a minimum there are over one million compulsive gamblers in the United States; treating some of them are the National Council on Compulsive Gambling, a group called Gamblers Anonymous, and special inpatient treatment wards in at least two Veterans Administration hospitals.[27]

For the most part the criminal justice system seems to ignore the crime of gambling, except where it is controlled by organized crime. Within the last few years, state governments have moved rapidly toward legalized gambling, unable to resist another source of revenue, regardless of any moral reservations. Thus with gambling we are seeing what is thought of as an abuse of a legally permissible activity, rather than the transference of a category of behavior from criminal justice to mental health. But it is quite clear from the program reports and the rhetoric employed in the discussion of compulsive gambling that a number of professionals think of it as a disease, with an identifiable cause and course—enough so that the American Psychiatric Association Task Force on Nomenclature is considering listing it in its next Diagnostic and Statistical Manual of Mental Disorders.

MENTAL RETARDATION

Mentally retarded offenders do not fit neatly into a discussion of the medicalization of deviance. They are generally held to have a diminished responsibility—they are thus not "bad," but yet not "sick" in the usual sense of the term. For the great majority of the retarded, medicine should play no greater role than it does within the general population, but it is the medical profession to which the legal profession turns for the solution of problems associated with mental deficiency. An association with mental illness is common, a dual diagnosis of retardation and mental illness is frequently made, and the retarded are frequently held in mental hospitals, as well as in prisons and institutions for the retarded.

The problem is not insignificant. It is estimated that 2 to 3 percent of the population is retarded (approximately five or six million people in the United States), with about 10 percent of the prison population consisting of individuals with some degree of retardation.[28] In some state prison systems the proportion of retarded inmates is as high as 30 percent, for a total estimate of 20,000 mentally retarded offenders nationally.

A current perspective on different approaches to the problem of the retarded offender can be found in a recent report sponsored by the President's Committee on Mental Retardation.[29] This volume contains a number of different recommendations as to how the problem should be handled.

On the one hand the committee calls for the establishment of a special court that would deal only with "exceptional offenders," and that would not be concerned with punishment, but only with the welfare of the individual.[30] The court would decide whether there was a gross intellectual deficit, and make an informal determination of whether the offense was committed. An affirmative finding on these two points would result in the court assuming supervisory powers, including the authority to commit to a specialized institution for an indeterminate period.

Others feel that this would be inappropriate and harmful.[31] Norval Morris, of the University of Chicago, objects to any special handling of retarded individuals on the grounds that the police power of the state should not be compromised by its mental health power. He argues that the mentally retarded suspect should receive exactly the same rights and protections as any other citizen, and that the incompetency plea and the defense of insanity should be abolished. Evidence of mental retardation would be pertinent only in regards to whether the defendant lacked the state of mind required as an element of the offense charged. Morris is concerned that any other treatment of the issue has much greater potential for harm than good. One such harm is illustrated by the following description of a courtroom scene:

> The judge was saying to the attorney, "I want to help your client. I think he can be rehabilitated and he should learn a trade. I am going to send him to the state penitentiary for five to fifteen years."
> The defense attorney jumped up and said, "Judge, this man cannot be rehabilitated. What he needs is punishment. Send him away for eleven and a half up to twenty-three months. He can never learn a trade."[32]

But the attorney who observed the above scene still would like to retain the option of pleading special conditions for the retarded offender. His position is that a defense attorney would like to have as many options as possible in getting the best possible deal for his client, observing that if the client can be put into treatment before trial, the charges are usually continued or dropped.

Once again, the major issue for debate is that of responsibility and the ultimate management of the offender. A review of the table of contents of *The Mentally Retarded Citizen and the Law* (Report of the President's Commission) suggests that much of the current thinking is clearly within a medical context. There is considerable concern with the provision of services, the right to habilitation, institutional standards, etc. These developments, which continue to place mental retardation in a health framework, coexist with the increased concern for due process for retarded offenders.

POLITICAL DISSENT

It is not possible to talk today about the use of psychiatry in controlling political dissent without immediately thinking about the Soviet Union. With the destalinization that occurred during the 1950s, the usual methods of dealing with dissent (purges, labor camps, and executions) were deemphasized. The resulting increase in public dissent called for new methods of control. In 1961, admission to a mental hospital was made easier, and later the psychiatric sector was given an official mandate to deal with political dissenters.[33] The law was amended in 1967 to allow psychiatric exams for practically anyone arrested on criminal charges. The misuse of psychiatry in this fashion has been so widely documented that even the World Psychiatric Association finally recognized the problem and passed a resolution condemning it. (The resolution was passed by a small majority at the 1977 meeting, after failures to do so at prior meetings.[34])

Accusations of a similar use of mental health professionals in the control of political deviance have been made against Rumania, East Germany, Argentina, Chile, South Africa, and the United Kingdom.[35] We have been less sensitive to the political uses of psychiatry in this country, and even though both the American Psychiatric Association and the American Psychological Association have formed committees to explore the problem, no work of significance has emerged.[36]

In the United States, political dissent has not been as directly labeled as a crime as it has in some other countries. Thus the notion that this particular form of deviance is being transferred from one control system to another is not as easily made as with some other forms of deviance. Yet there are some well-known examples. Thomas Szasz has written in detail regarding the treatment of Ezra Pound and General Edwin Walker.[37] I have described elsewhere the experiences of a Florida activist, Jim Fair, who was committed to a mental hospital because of his troublesome behavior.[38]

Equally pertinent to the issue at hand is Bruno Bettelheim's character- ization of student protesters of the 1960s as "very sick [and in] need not of police action but psychiatric care," and the interpretation advanced by neurosurgeons that brain dysfunction in participants in ghetto disorders may have been as strong a reason for the disorders as were the social and economic causes.[39] These last two instances reflect the characterization of entire groups of people, rather than individuals, as pathological, thus neutralizing the impact of their statements and actions by moving them from the political to the medical arena. It follows then that it is the individual who is to be changed, rather than the social structure. This point was made recently by an Anglican priest who had fasted for sixty-three days to protest the treatment of political detainees in South Africa:

> Terrible things are being done in a bid to make me break my fast. I have reliable information that measures are being taken in an attempt to have me certified insane. My informants tell me that the idea is that if I can be put away in an asylum I will lose any status as a protester I might have gained through my protest.[40]

I do not know if attempts were made to have the priest committed, but there can be no question about the validity of his conclusions.

The subtle use of psychiatry as control is further illustrated in a conflict between a professor and his university administration. In June of 1977, Edgar Beall, a tenured professor of physics at the University of Maryland, was suspended from teaching and told that he could not return to the classroom unless he could get a psychiatrist to certify to university health officials that he wasn't a "threat to [him]self or others" and that he was able "to meet [his] university responsibilities."[41] The year's suspension occurred without a hearing or publicly disclosed charges, but supposedly followed an altercation with a fellow faculty member. The case also has political overtones: Beall is reported to be a long-time social activist and critic (protesting the war in Vietnam, university investments with firms doing business with South Africa, etc.), and a supporter of Mao Tse-tung. Beall declined to see a psy- chiatrist on the grounds that "my passing the test would not guarantee my personal safety and my acquiescence could lay the groundwork for actions against others." Subsequently, Beall was served with a specific set of charges, and dismissal proceedings were set in motion.

I have not met Professor Beall, and my knowledge of the situation is limited to what has appeared in the newspaper. As far as I know, he may be exceedingly competent, or he may be a cantankerous, incompetent person who has failed to do his job and should not be in the classroom. University officials may have acted in good faith. But regardless of the competence or incompetence of Professor Beall, they did not act wisely. Requiring a psychiatric examination as a condition of continuance in a job raises questions about the competence of the individual in a way that casts doubt on the person's beliefs, political and otherwise, regardless of the outcome of the psychiatric report. More importantly, it asks the psychiatrist to provide assurances that he or she has no business giving. It is not possible to certify with any accuracy that a person is not a threat to himself, or herself or to others, and no technical basis exists in psychiatry for determining that an individual is "able to meet university responsibilities." There are other criteria for evaluating job performance that should be employed; presumably the university is now pressing its case on these other grounds.

Other examples of the medicalization of political behavior can be found in the daily papers, even though the transfer process is frequently ambiguous. Psychiatrists are frequently brought in to determine the issue of responsibility, and they usually argue nonresponsibility—as in the cases of Squeaky Fromme, Lee Oswald, Patty Hearst, and the "Son of Sam." The issue frequently becomes complicated, as in the Patty Hearst case, in which it is uncertain whether or not she was involved in ideologically based crimes, essentially political in nature, or whether she was brainwashed.

My purpose here is simply to illustrate another category of behavior that illustrates the overall theme of the continuing expansion of behaviors subject to control through the mental health system. But before leaving this topic, it is worth noting that modern China appears to be moving in the opposite direction. There, it seems to be close to official doctrine that mental illness is perceived as a political problem, and psychotic deviants are turned over to Maoist politicians for political reeducation;[42] it is assumed that self-criticism will make them politically active and thus healthy.

CHILD ABUSE

Before the 1960s there was very little public concern over serious maltreatment of children. But once public awareness was aroused, things moved very quickly. In 1974 Congress passed the Child Abuse Prevention and Treatment Act, which contained a proposed model for state adoption. All fifty states now have mandatory reporting laws (under penalty of criminal sanction) that require a variety of professionals to report all "suspected" cases of child abuse or neglect to public welfare officials.[43] Florida, as an example, had over 90,000 complaints during the first three years that its system was in operation, with well over 60 percent of all cases confirmed as valid under an extremely broad statute.[44]

This subject can be a particularly helpful one for our analysis because it illustrates a number of the problems common to other instances of the medicalization of deviance.

1. The approach in the federal legislation (and thus in the states) and in an independently proposed model system is clearly therapeutic and rehabilitative in orientation. The goal is to bring suspected child abusers into diagnosis and treatment through a medical track, with law enforcement officers and protective service workers disqualified as primary gatekeepers. The following quotes are illustrative:

> The concept of a state responsibility to rehabilitate is a growing one, and it has recently been formalized by the idea that statutes for termination of parental rights include a familial right to treatment philosophy.[45]

> The strategy of the model system is to take the calculated risk of further empowering medical institutions in the area of child abuse decision-making in order to enhance their "counter-vailing power" in relation to the justice system. In basic political and institutional terms this strategy is a major aim of model system development.[46]

> The role of the caseworker is the key to what will happen in the abuse case. His/her decision will determine services given, removal of the child from the home, and justice system involvement.[47]

2. Social control systems tend to be expansive with respect to the range of behaviors subject to their control. This is a part of the natural history of bureaucracies and control systems. And so it is with respect to child abuse. The trend has been to broaden the types of professionals mandated to report, and the definition of reportable child abuse. Initial concerns dealt only with the "battered child" or physical abuse. But, under the Child Abuse Prevention and Treatment Act, the definition of abuse has been expanded to include:

> the physical or mental injury, sexual abuse, negligent treatment, or maltreatment of a child under the age of eighteen by a person who is responsible for the child's welfare under circumstances which indicate that

the child's health or welfare is harmed or threatened thereby, as determined in accordance with regulations prescribed by the Secretary.[48]

In Virginia, the following has been included in the definition of abuse:

Emotional neglect; listless/tired with no apparent reason; moral neglect; exposed to unwholesome and demoralizing circumstances; denied normal experience that produce [sic] feelings of being loved, wanted, secure and worthy.[49]

It is clear from the above that the definition of abuse is so broad that intrusion into family life could be justified in almost any situation. If recent figures from Virginia[50] and Florida[51] are representative of the nation as a whole, then only 8 to 10 percent of the confirmed cases deal with physical abuse, meaning the system is dealing primarily with lesser forms of family dysfunction. It should be noted that the model system proposed by Arnold Schuchter recognizes the problems of overexpansion and would restrict intervention to instances of physical abuse.[52]

3. The professional frequently is involved in multiple roles that involve mixed allegiances. The child abuse worker is particularly subject to ambiguity and confusion in the course of dealing with families. The worker has the responsibility of helping the abusing parent, the power to remove the child from the home, and the opportunity to contribute to prosecution. It is not likely that all three of these functions can be carried out simultaneously. To be entirely fair, the worker would need to tell the parent about the multiple roles during the initial contact. Revealing that kind of information would not instill the trust necessary to an effective therapeutic relationship. This is a major problem for the mental health worker in any situation involving coercion, but particularly so with respect to child abuse.

It should be noted that physicians have been a part of the social control system in that for a number of years they have been required to report drug abuse, gunshot wounds, and suicide attempts. Under a recent court decision these duties have been extended to include liability for injuries inflicted by a third party, when the physician fails to diagnose child abuse and the child is subsequently injured.[53]

4. The threat of criminal prosecution can be used to coerce abusing parents into treatment. This situation is analogous to circumstances frequently surrounding admission to a mental hospital. The patient is given a choice—enter voluntarily or be committed. The choice for the suspected abusing parent is that of entering treatment or facing the threat of loss of the child and criminal prosecution—a power that many consider necessary in order to provide treatment. On the other hand, there is a widespread feeling that treatment offered under coercive conditions is not likely to be successful.[54] The mere possibility of removal of the child or criminal prosecution can be coercive even in due-process or civil-libertarian models where the treatment services are supposed to be truly voluntary.

5. *The objects of investigation tend to be the poor.* This has been true for the majority of people handled by the criminal justice, mental health, and welfare systems. But here again, it is particularly true with respect to child abuse, even though there is a widely held belief that the problem is common across all social classes. The research on child abuse has concentrated primarily on lower socioeconomic groups; the population most vulnerable to being reported has included people using public hospitals and clinics, and people on welfare, all of whom are subject to social work contact or supervision. Those able to use private physicians and hospitals are much less likely to be reported.

6. *The focus tends to be on the pathology of the individual, rather than on contributing social conditions.* As with most situations involving the medicalization of deviance, the problem is usually defined as pathology within the individual and corrective action tends to be directed at the individual.[55] When the 10 percent of the cases that involve physical abuse are set aside, some interesting questions can be raised about the remaining. Recall, for example, some of the definitions in the Virginia system. Could "listless/tired with no apparent reason" be related to crowded conditions in the home or to an inadequate diet? What enters into a caseworker's judgment that the child is being "exposed to unwholesome and demoralizing circumstances"? What are the causes and meaning of "moral neglect"? And so on. It seems probable that at least some of the causes and remedies might lie in events external to the "abusing parent"—e.g., improvements in welfare support and health care; or the provision of universal day care.

The legitimacy of a state interest in the welfare of children cannot be questioned, particularly where there has been severe physical abuse, but the hazards of coercive intervention need to be recognized. Current programs have resulted in the identification of massive numbers of individuals suspected of child abuse. And although the intent of the interveners is benevolent and humane, it seems likely that opposite outcomes are achieved in many instances. The available evidence indicates strongly that foster placement of children and attempts at control may well result in more harm than good, and in greater rather than lesser family instability. In this instance the transfer from the criminal justice system to the mental health system has probably brought a large number of people under surveillance who would have been better off outside of both systems.

ADDITIONAL EXAMPLES

There is virtually no limit to the kinds of behaviors subject to medicalization, and thus far I have dealt only with categories where the shift has been relatively dramatic. A number of additional disparate behaviors and situations exist in which the mental health system is playing an expanded role. The courts, in both formal and informal ways, ask mental health professionals to aid in questions involving the insanity defense, competence to stand trial, custody decisions, and sentencing.

Socially and politically significant people who are charged with criminal offenses are particularly likely to make use of medical authority as a means of ameliorating their situation. Florida provides interesting examples of the courts' use of the mental health expert. Within the last few years, the mental health system has been asked to aid the state's courts in the disposition of problems presented by a number of public figures: (1) whether a state supreme court justice was sufficiently emotionally stable to serve on the court; (2) whether a former state treasurer could stand trial on charges of tax evasion, and if shock therapy would interfere with the trial; (3) whether another resigned cabinet member (state comptroller) could stand trial; (4) what disposition should be made of a state cabinet member (superintendent of education) who had pled guilty to charges of bribery. (Florida, incidentally, is not being singled out because of its particularly corrupt leaders, but only because it is the situation with which I am most familiar. There are parallels in most other states.)

The courts are particularly prone to call on mental health professionals when the offender has acted "out of character." For example, the District of Columbia Court of Appeals recently upheld the sentence of a city council member who had assaulted a tow truck driver who was blocking the entrance to a parking lot.[56] In the assault, the council member had bitten the other man three times, behavior that the probation officer and the judge found to be peculiar in a well-educated professional. Thus he was required to undergo a mental examination, and if necessary, to receive psychiatric or psychological treatment. The appeals court rejected the council member's argument that the order for the psychiatric examination was beyond the judge's authority, stating that the conditions of probation are up to the judge's discretion.

One reason shoplifting is receiving consideration as a sickness may be found in the quality of the offender. Apparently the average customer is responsible for most of the stealing, and a district court judge in Cambridge, Massachusetts, has noted a surprising number of shoplifting attempts by members of the academic community.[57] Many of these individuals do not regard themselves as dishonest or disturbed, but rather as someone taking a little something from an impersonal corporation. But the trend to define it as a sickness of sorts has gone far enough so that Chicago recently opened a shoplifting court that has immediate access to a social service department and counseling services.[58]

The list goes on. Rape, spouse abuse, and suicide are criminal offenses frequently thought to reflect sickness. So, while there is some talk of demedicalization, the evidence for such a movement is limited at this point, and the trend seems to be in the reverse direction.

NOTES

1. Progress and Problems in Treating Alcohol Abusers. Report to the Congress by the Comptroller General of the United States, April 1977.
2. Erskine, H. and Bryant, S. An evaluation of the effect of alcohol programs on alcohol-related crime. Unpublished paper.
3. Ibid.
4. *Congressional Quarterly,* 1977, p. 853.
5. Public Law 94–371.
6. Progress and Problems in Treating Alcohol Abusers.
7. *Los Angeles Times,* December 6, 1977.
8. Kind, R. The American System: Legal Sanctions to Repress Drug Abuse. In Inciardi, J. A. and Chambers, C. D. (eds.), *Drugs and the Criminal Justice System.* Sage, 1974.
9. Interview with Peter Bourne, *Atlanta Constitution,* October 25, 1977.
10. Taborg, M. A., Levin, D. R., Milkmon, R. H., and Center, L. J. Treatment Alternatives to Street Crime. National Evaluation Program, Phase I, Summary Report. National Institute of Law Enforcement, Law Enforcement Assistance Administration, U.S. Department of Justice.
11. Miller, K. S., Miller, E. T., and Schmidt, W. Diversion of Drug Offenders from the Criminal Justice System—An Evaluation of the Baumgartner Act. Report submitted to the Florida Department of Health and Rehabilitative Services, Drug Abuse Program, 1977.
12. *National Drug Reporter,* December, 1977.
13. See notes 10 and 11.
14. President's Commission on Mental Health. Vol. IV, U.S. Government Printing Office, 1978, p. 2123.
15. Ibid., p. 2122
16. *Washington Post,* December 18, 1977.
17. Ibid.
18. *Tallahassee Democrat,* April 18, 1978.

19. *Washington Post,* May 16, 1978.
20. Neier, A. *Crime and Punishment.* Stein and Day, 1976, pp. 25–26.
21. Gish v. Board of Education of Bor. of Paramus, etc., 366 A. 2d 1337, N.J. App. (1976).
22. Gaylord v. Tacoma School District No. 10, 559 1/4 2d 1340, Washington (1976).
23. Torrey, E. F. *The Death of Psychiatry.* Penguin Books, 1975, pp. 43–44.
24. House Bill #1569, 1977 session of the Florida legislature.
25. *Civil Commitment of Special Categories of Offenders.* National Institute of Mental Health, Center for the Studies of Crime and Delinquency, 1971.
26. The compulsive gambler. *Today in Psychiatry* (Abbott Laboratories), 1977, 3, No. 4, April, p. 1.
27. Satchell, M., A hospital that helps gamblers kick the habit. *Parade,* January 15, 1978, p. 26; *Tallahassee Democrat,* June 14, 1977.
28. Brown and Courtless. Penal and correctional institutions. *American Journal of Psychiatry,* 1968, p. 1164. Cited in Kindred, M., Cohen, J., Penrod, D. and Shaffer, T. *The Mentally Retarded Citizen and the Law.* Free Press, 1976.
29. Kindred et al., *The Mentally Retarded Citizen and the Law.*
30. Ibid., p. 636 ff.
31. Morris, N. Special Doctrinal Treatment in Criminal Law, in Kindred et al., *The Mentally Retarded Citizen and the Law;* Wald, P. Basic Personal and Civil Rights, in Kindred et al., *The Mentally Retarded Citizen and the Law.*
32. Kindred et al., *The Mentally Retarded Citizen and the Law,* p. 688.
33. Conrad, P. Soviet dissidents, ideological deviance and mental hospitalization. Paper presented at the annual meeting of the Midwest Sociological Society, April 14, 1977.
34. Reddaway, P., and Bloch, S. Curbing psychiatry's political misuse. *Washington Post,* November 15, 1977.
35. Ibid.
36. Miller, K. S. *Managing Madness.* Free Press, 1976, pp. 124–125.
37. Szasz, T. S. *Law, Liberty, and Psychiatry: An Inquiry into the Social Uses of Mental Health Practices.* Macmillan, 1963, pp. 199–211.
38. Miller, K. S. *Managing Madness,* pp. 26–35.
39. Conrad, P. Soviet Dissidents.
40. *London Times,* October 22, 1971.
41. *Washington Post,* May 12, 1978.
42. Illich, I. *Medical Nemesis.* Pantheon, 1976, p. 164.
43. DeFrancis, V., and Lucht, C. L. *Child Abuse Legislation in the 1970's.* American Humane Association, Children's Division, 1974.
44. Schuchter, A. *Child Abuse Intervention.* National Institute of Law Enforcement and Criminal Justice, Law Enforcement Assistance Administration, U.S. Department of Justice, 1976, p. 13. This is an excellent comprehensive reference to the literature on child abuse.
45. Derdeyn, A. P. Child abuse and neglect: The rights of parents and the needs of their children. *American Journal of Orthopsychiatry,* 1977, 47, 382.
46. Schuchter, *Child Abuse Intervention,* p. 59.
47. Ibid., p. 6.
48. Child Abuse Prevention and Treatment Act (P.L. 93–247).
49. Virginia Department of Welfare, Bureau of Protective Services, *Annual Report,* 1975–1976. Cited by S. W. Bricker in testimony on the Child Abuse Prevention and Treatment Act, before the U.S. Senate Subcommittee on Child and Human Development, April 7, 1977.
50. Ibid.
51. Schuchter, *Child Abuse Prevention,* p. 13.

52. Ibid., p. 26.
53. Curran, W. J. Failure to diagnose battered-child syndrome. *The New England Journal of Medicine*, 1977, 296, 795–796.
54. Wald, M. State intervention on behalf of 'neglected' children: a search for realistic standards. *Stanford Law Review*, 1975, 27, 985–1040.
55. Gelles, R. Child abuse as psychopathology: a sociological critique and reformulation. *American Journal of Orthopsychiatry*, 1973, 43, 3.
56. *Washington Post*, May 16, 1978.
57. Krantz, S., Smith, C., Rossman, D., Froyd, P., and Hoffman, J. *Right to Counsel in Criminal Cases: The Mandate of Argersinger v. Hamlin*. Ballinger, 1976, pp. 590–591.
58. *St. Petersburg Times*, April 19, 1976.

Chapter 3

The Therapeutic State and Current Court Cases

Judicial involvement in the public practice of psychiatry is a recent development. One of the nation's best known mental health attorneys, Bruce Ennis, states that as recently as 1968 he could have covered the subject in a few pages, and that he had participated personally in a majority of the cases.[1] Ten years later there are hundreds of cases on patients' rights pending in state and federal courts; for the first time in this country the U.S. Supreme Court has ruled on the rights of a civilly committed mental patient; the American Bar Association has found it necessary to publish a monthly *Mental Disability Law Reporter;* and federal judges have abandoned, in a dramatic way, their long-held "hands-off" policy regarding mental patients. As Bruce Ennis states, "The rapidity and the extent of this change in judicial attitudes are astonishing and, to my knowledge, unprecedented. In no other area of the law of which I am aware has so much changed, so fast."[2] Ennis goes on to point out that this represents a complete turnabout from the period between 1955 and 1970, when the "medical model" dominated psychiatric practice.

Note: This chapter was coauthored by Kent S. Miller, Sara Beck Fein, and Winsor Schmidt.

Many of the court decisions expanding the rights of mental patients have been based on the recent recognition that, in given instances, the values assigned to personal freedom and autonomy may outweigh mental health values. There has also been an increased awareness that much of what goes on within the mental health system is more art than science.

Disillusionment and concern about the disease model as it applies to a wide range of deviance is now being reflected in court decisions. Judge David Bazelon, a longtime member of the U.S. Court of Appeals in Washington, D.C., has been an active supporter and friend of the mental health professions. Many of the major court decisions relating to mental health, including the right to treatment, have come out of his court. But he is now a major critic of the mental health professions, and is much concerned about the failure and abuses that he has seen over the years. In *Washington* v. *United States,* he adopted a former dissenting argument and prohibited psychiatrists from testifying about the conclusive legal label of whether an alleged offense was a "product" of mental illness in the application of the Durham-McDonald insanity test.[3] Bazelon noted that if "psychiatry and the other social and behavioral sciences cannot provide sufficient data relevant to a determination of criminal responsibility" with the new rule of evidence limiting the use of conclusive legal labels, then it might be necessary to abolish the insanity defense, "or refashion it in a way which is not tied so closely to the medical model."[4]

A year later, Bazelon reversed a dismissal of a habeas corpus writ by an appellant who was subjected to a sexual psychopath statute when the trial court did not distinguish between sexual and nonsexual misconduct as a basis for commitment, and when the trial court also neglected to determine the likelihood rather than the mere possibility of sexual misbehavior.[5] In relating the origin of the Sexual Psychopath Act, Bazelon remarked that in 1948 it was not "senseless to invoke the medical model and provide for the hospitalization of a class of persons [sexual psychopaths] who were not 'insane.' "[6] Bazelon cited the broadening of the District of Columbia insanity test in *Durham* v. *United States*[7] and *McDonald* v. *United States*[8] to suggest that the 1948 Sexual Psychopath Act was no longer distinct from the medical model of criminal responsibility, or else was an inane expansion of the medical model to a class that was not insane.

The District of Columbia has continued to struggle with the medical model,[9] joined periodically by expressions of concern in other jurisdictions.[10] More recently, one federal court has expressly returned "to the 'legal model' as opposed to the 'medical model' in civil commitment cases," relying upon the "overriding consideration behind recent cases . . . that personal freedom is involved" and "that the diagnosis and treatment of mental illness leave too much to subjective choices by less than neutral individuals."[11] The court observed that the law that it struck down, relating to "Mental Health, Mental Illness, Drug Addiction and Alcoholism," had "adopted the 'medical model' and repealed the 'legal model' in dealing with persons who behave differently than their peers because of some mental disorder or because of the intake of drugs or alcohol."[12] The court stated that the impetus for challenge to the law hailed in 1968 and 1969 "as a progressive and liberal piece of legislation" was not so much patient mistreatment as it was:

> a growing disillusionment with the 'medical model' in all fields of behavioral control of human beings, the impact of recent decisions of federal courts, and the ongoing skepticism of civil libertarians with all forms of enforced assistance.[13]

These illustrative court decisions are frequently cited as evidence of a move away from the therapeutic state and the medical model. But this sampling of court opinion may not be an accurate reflection of the trend within a broader context. Our purpose in this chapter is to conduct a more detailed review of current court decisions as they relate to various aspects of the therapeutic state. There are other avenues for such an audit—e.g., legislation or positions being taken by professional groups—but since the courts are now playing a prominent role in this field, a review of their actions should prove instructive.

Such an analysis has obvious dangers and limitations and these should be recognized at the outset. We noted above that judicial activity in this area is expanding rapidly, and that it is simply not possible to stay abreast of all of it. We have focused primarily on a narrow period of time —1975 through 1977—and observers of the United States Supreme Court can readily attest that courts can change directions quickly. There is a further source of error in that cases that have been filed but not decided have been included on the grounds that something is to be learned from a consideration of the issues that are being brought to the court with some expectation of redress. In addition, we have included decisions from courts with differing levels of authority.

As always, there are points at which those with a perspective different from ours would arrive at different conclusions. We, of course, are persuaded that the analysis that follows is valid. There is no pretension to have reviewed all decisions that speak to the issues under consideration, but since our purpose is to search for trends, this is not a major problem. We have attempted to be comprehensive and have included every case that we could discover that seemed to relate to the basic theme in one way or another. The primary focus on 1975–1977 was an attempt to limit the search to a manageable time frame that would reflect current trends.

THE RIGHT TO TREATMENT

The right to treatment, a legal concept that is less than twenty years old, has played a major role in the expansion of the therapeutic state. It has provided an explicit tie between the law and therapy, and has legitimized diverse elements of the therapeutic system by requiring treatment in instances where a person might otherwise be incarcerated, thus increasing the need for therapeutic services. Although the Supreme Court in *Donaldson* v. *O'Connor* deliberately avoided dealing with the right to treatment aspects of the case, lower courts have consistently affirmed the right to individualized treatment for a wide range of problems and in a variety of settings, on both statutory and constitutional grounds.[14] Frequently it has been included with a number of other rights, including the concept of the least restrictive alternative, the right to education and work programs, and protection from harm.

If anything, the courts have tended to be expansive and to integrate the various rights into a general web. For example, the protection from harm concept has been interpreted to include the development of programs for residents of institutions on the grounds that "harm can result not only from neglect but from conditions which cause regression or which prevent the development of an individual's capability."[15] It has also been ruled that treatment must be provided not only while the person is a resident of a mental hospital but also upon return to the community.[16]

A further illustration of the tendency to expand the net can be seen in a court's interpretation of a diversion statute for narcotics offenders. Supervisory treatment was deemed to have been intended to include not only those who regularly used narcotics, but also for "prospective users, early stage users or experimenters, even though such persons ought not necessarily require the type of supervisory treatment called for by those who are regular users or addicts."[17]

The states have not been particularly resistant to right to treatment suits, as reflected by the suits' being frequently settled with a consent decree. Mental health officials have been somewhat ambivalent, hoping that the courts will order additional resources for the institutions, a hope that has been only partially met. Although in some instances budgets have increased dramatically, most state institutions have been so badly neglected for such a long time that significant change could come only as a result of a radical shift in state legislatures' priorities. The courts have recognized this reality, and in many right to treatment cases they have retained jurisdiction and established special review panels to oversee the implementation of rulings. It is also not unusual for the courts to resort to the threat or the use of contempt actions.[18]

It should be noted that not all of the litigants in right to treatment cases would like to see additional resources poured into state institutions. The people in this camp realize that the state is not likely to commit enough money for compliance with court orders, and they hope that the continued pressure will result in the institutions being dismantled. Thus it was that some of the parties to *O'Connor* v. *Donaldson* were pleased when the court refused to review it as a right to treatment case; being generally opposed to civil commitment, their concern was that requiring the state to provide treatment might justify sending more people to the hospitals.

Sooner or later the Supreme Court will have to deal with the variety of issues subsumed under the right to treatment. At this time, the lower courts seem to have no doubt that such a right exists. Their rulings are consistent with, and give support to, the idea that much deviant behavior constitutes sickness subject to control through treatment, and that the state has an obligation to provide treatment. There seems to be a growing awareness that this principle holds regardless of whether the patient or inmate is voluntary or involuntary.[19]

Treatment in the Prisons

Many of those closely associated with the criminal justice system have called for the system's withdrawal from the rehabilitation business altogether. In making just such a call, the director of the U.S. Justice Department's Bureau of Prisons said:

> The concept of rehabilitation fits not only our religious beliefs about the perfectability of mankind, but also our utilitarian desire to reduce the impact of crime by preventing crime at the source . . . . The vast majority of offenders have no serious mental disease or defect. Crime may be a plague on society, but it is not a disease for which we have a guaranteed cure.[20]

It was noted in Chapter 1 that Norman Carlson has considerable support for the idea that the prisons should abandon the medical model and coerced treatment, and indeed there are those who believe that this perspective has carried the day. But there is important evidence for the opposite view. The argument is now being made that the failure of treatment and rehabilitative efforts has not been documented as well as some would claim. It is claimed that many assessments have been global, when in fact there is a need to talk about specific treatments applied to specific types of prisoners. A more telling argument is that treatment has never really been available in the prisons—witness the extremely small number of personnel that could be considered to be giving treatment even under a liberal definition of the term, particularly in light of recent studies showing that a high percentage of jail and prison inmates are mentally handicapped.[21]

Federal judge Frank Johnson has observed that the mental disability system is being drawn increasingly into meeting the mental health needs of persons caught in the criminal justice system, including convicted criminals. Recent court decisions strongly support this conclusion. In our review we found only one court decision that was not consistent with the trend to require rehabilitation programs in the prison system. In *Bresolin v. Morris*, the Supreme Court of the state of Washington denied the request of an inmate to have a drug treatment program established.[22] The court held that there was no fundamental right to rehabilitation at public expense after conviction of a crime, and denied that drug treatment was a part of reasonable medical care. There were also two cases in which the language of the court suggested moderation: one in which the court cautioned that treatment was limited by cost and time factors, and that the test should be one of medical necessity, not what might be considered desirable;[23] and a second instance in which a superior court ruled that the state was not required to place a juvenile offender in a psychiatric hospital at an expense of $40,000 per year.[24] These are the exceptions to a number of rulings supporting therapeutic/rehabilitative practice.

Current decisions have mandated that mentally retarded or emotionally disturbed prisoners are entitled to appropriate treatment, either within or outside the prison.[25] The Washington Supreme Court held that the state must provide the pay for habilitative services (in a private facility if necessary) for a twice convicted offender who was, at most, mildly mentally retarded.[26] In states as far apart as Alabama and New Hampshire, the right to treatment for imprisoned individuals has been defined as a constitutional right, and "the prisons are under an affirmative duty to provide same."[27] This requirement has even been extended to a county jail, in which it was required that detoxification and psychiatric treatment services be provided on an emergency and regular basis.[28]

The notion that rehabilitation is an appropriate function in prisons is clearly illustrated in the finding that a federal prisoner could be disciplined for refusing to participate in a compulsory education program. In this particular instance, the prisoner had refused to spell words out loud in a classroom.[29] The court held that if participation in such programs could be at the option of the prisoner, it would defeat the very purpose of rehabilitation.

In several additional cases, the courts have continued to maintain an interest in general treatment conditions in prisons and training schools. This interest has included a concern for individual treatment programs,[30] personnel to provide treatment,[31] the provision of treatment in order to qualify a prisoner for parole,[32] and the development of treatment programs for specific problems (e.g., alcoholism).[33] In most instances, the decisions have been based on the Eighth and Fourteenth Amendments.

The courts have also been involved in the movement of individuals between prisons and mental hospitals, primarily to guarantee due process protections. It is generally assumed that such transfers are commonplace, and in some jurisdictions they are treated as mere administrative "placement and classification" decisions.[34] The President's Commission on Mental Health points out that "a number of cases have held that because of the possibility of mistake, stigma, and lengthier confinement, a prisoner who is to be involuntarily transferred to a mental hospital should first be granted a civil commitment-type hearing."[35] The few applicable rulings during the period covered in this report reflect this concern over safeguards.

In a West Virginia case, the court found, among other things, that a prisoner was inappropriately transferred and that his exclusion from a federally funded vocational rehabilitation program in the prison because of mental illness violated the 1973 Rehabilitation Act.[36] It was noted that individuals transferred are not required to be released upon expiration of the sentence, and that parole hearings are not offered to those in the hospital. On the other hand, an appellate court in New York reversed a district court decision holding that the state had been violating the Fourteenth Amendment in its method of returning mental patients to prison.[37] The higher court found that the decision to "dehospitalize" an inmate was purely a medical decision and did not call for the requested due process feature. (The chief judge dissented, saying that the majority "glossed over the clear implication of the record that officials at the hospital have regularly returned mentally ill patients to prison for punitive reasons, to languish in solitary confinement without even a semblance of medical care.")

In summary, to the extent that the courts have much to say about treatment and rehabilitation programs within the prison system, such programs will continue. It seems probable that safeguards will increase, and that treatment will be less coercive and more clearly divorced from decisions about release from prison, but that the notion of treatment and rehabilitation will continue. These developments have occurred in a brief span of time, since as recently as 1974 a reviewer of case law stated that the argument that committed criminals have a right to treatment had not been accepted, despite recommendations to that effect by various advisory groups.[38]

An increase in court activity can be expected if a bill now in Congress is passed. This bill would allow the U.S. Justice Department to intervene in suits against state institutions, a practice that was in effect until a federal district court ruled in 1976 that there was no statutory authority to enter such suits. The Justice Department argues that it needs this authority to "embark on a coordinated program of litigation." In view of the Justice Department's history on this issue, it is reasonable to suggest that their approach will strongly support a therapeutic state orientation.

THE RIGHT TO REFUSE TREATMENT

Not unexpectedly, as the right to treatment has been brought to issue in an increasing variety of situations, the right to refuse treatment, as a logical balance, has also begun to develop as a legal concept. As recently as 1974 a reviewer stated "judicial acceptance of the argument that involuntarily confined individuals have the right to refuse unwanted treatment remains largely unrealized, but advocates of such a thesis may point to several recent cases as support for their argument."[39] Pertinent cases since that time have centered around two issues. One of these is the question of when informed consent is required before treatment may be administered, an issue occurring often in conjunction with situations that require appointment of guardians, and with the procedures through which a guardian may decide on treatment issues. A second issue is when treatment may be imposed over the objections of the patient, including the question of whether procedures labelled "treatment" may be used for purposes of control and punishment. The courts have additionally, in some cases, described what must be involved for consent to be considered "informed."

Although the U.S. Constitution does not expressly provide a right to refuse treatment, and thus far no court has invoked such a constitutional right, there does seem to be sufficient precedent to predict ultimate judicial recognition of such a right.[40] The constitutional arguments for the right to refuse treatment have been based on a range of provisions, including (1) the right to privacy and autonomy, (2) the cruel and unusual punishment prohibition of the Eighth Amendment, (3) the right to freedom of expression, (4) religious grounds, and (5) the equal protection clause (under which *physically* ill persons are allowed to decide whether or not to accept treatment).[41]

A major focus of court decisions has been the distinction between "intrusive" therapies (such as psychosurgery and electroconvulsive therapy) and "common medical practice." In *Price* v. *Sheppard*, the Minnesota Supreme Court ruled that before intrusive therapies can be applied to unwilling mental patients, an appropriate county court must appoint a guardian for the patient.[42] Such therapy must be found by the court to be "reasonable and necessary" in order for the state to assume the decision to administer it. However, the same court, overturning a lower court that had ruled that use of the drug Prolixin was an intrusive therapy, decided that the *Price* v. *Sheppard* protections did not extend to Prolixin because it is common medical practice.[43] It thus distinguished the protections given to unwilling patients according to intrusiveness or commonness of the proposed therapy.

Two courts have upheld the right of patients not to be subjected to electroconvulsive therapy, psychosurgery, aversive reinforcement conditioning, or other unusual or hazardous procedures without their informed consent after consultation with counsel or an interested party of the patient's choice.[44] Informed consent has been defined as "the uncoerced decision of a resident who has comprehension and can signify assent or dissent."[45] Both of these courts distinguished between competent and incompetent patients.

Further elaborating the concept of informed consent, a Michigan circuit court has ruled that informed consent to experimental procedures is not possible for involuntarily confined mental patients.[46] The court delineated three basic elements required before consent could be considered informed: competency, knowledge, and voluntariness. It stated that incarceration diminishes competency; knowledge of experimental procedures is nonexistent; and consent from an involuntary patient cannot be truly voluntary. Therefore, even though the patient and his parents had consented to experimental brain surgery, the court ruled that the procedure could not be carried out.

Since the use of drugs in institutional settings is so widespread as to include almost every patient, it is not surprising that many of the right to refuse treatment cases have centered around forced medication. Three recent federal court decisions have held that patient's complaints that they were given psychoactive medications without their consent are grounds for federal action.[47] It has also been held that a competent person objecting on religious grounds cannot be forced to accept non-emergency medication,[48] and at least one additional case involving a patient's right to refuse medication on religious grounds has been filed.[49]

There have been several recent rulings regarding the use of procedures generally considered therapy as punishment. In a case still pending, a U.S. district court in Pennsylvania has ruled that the involuntary administration of drugs that have a painful or frightening effect can amount to cruel and unusual punishment.[50] Two court decisions have held that therapy used primarily for control of patients[51] and for control of confined juveniles[52] violates the Constitution. On appeal to the First Circuit Court of Appeals is a case seeking the right of both involuntary and voluntary patients to refuse psychotropic drugs forcibly administered for punishment.[53]

Without enjoining the use of drugs for punishment, two other court decisions have established procedural safeguards regarding this use of drugs. A U.S. federal district court in New York required a judicial hearing to determine the mental or emotional instability of women prisoners before they could be transferred to a hospital for the criminally insane and be forced to participate in a psychiatric behavioral program.[54] The program included forced medication and deprivations without any valid medical purpose, both imposed as punishment without a hearing. Another court made informed consent a condition for continuing the use of a vomit-inducing drug as punishment. Patients could consent if the physician authorized every shot and if the rule violation for which the drug was administered had been witnessed by a staff member rather than solely by a fellow inmate. Consent, in writing, had to be subject to revocation by the patient at any time.[55]

Courts have exercised the authority to order treatment over the objection of minors,[56] and to order the withholding of treatment from incompetent persons even when the treatment would extend the life of the person concerned.[57] The patient in this latter case was a sixty-seven year-old profoundly retarded person with acute leukemia for which there is no treatment that would extend life beyond a few weeks or months. In the former case, a trial court in New Jersey ruled that electroprod therapy was necessary therapy for a minor whose special classes and outpatient treatment had failed to control her head-banging behavior. The case is on appeal.

Several cases have indicated methods the courts will use to implement or enforce the right to refuse treatment. These include, generally, both damages against individuals and the setting up of structures to enforce the patients' rights.

Some of the safeguarding structures have already been mentioned, such as the written consent as part of the patients' files and the requirement that physicians authorize every shot of a vomit-inducing drug. In another pending case that may set up a safeguarding structure, a Mississippi district court has found there is an issue as to whether physicians have followed the regulations they themselves set up concerning consent for intrusive treatment, including electroconvulsive therapy. The plaintiffs are additionally challenging the procedure by which the determination of competency to give consent is made solely by the attending physician.[58]

The Massachusetts Psychiatric Society has submitted an amicus curiae brief concerning controls on the use of seclusion and psychotropic drugs for objecting state hospital residents.[59] The society argued that the treatment decision should be made by the hospital staff, but that the next best alternative would be the establishment of a treatment review board similar to the extraordinary treatment committees established in the *Wyatt* v. *Stickney* case.

A second type of enforcement procedure is the seeking of damages from persons in authority for the imposition of treatment without consent. Two recent cases have sought damages for the use of electroconvulsive therapy without the patient's consent. In one instance, damages were awarded to a patient who sustained multiple injuries through electroconvulsive therapy, administered despite his complaints of pain.[60] After four treatments in a one-week period, the plaintiff, who had had a complete physical examination before admission to the hospital, was found to have fractures of his thoracic vertebrae, both shoulder joints, and both hip joints. He was awarded $35,000, one-third to be paid by the state as employer of the nurses, and two-thirds to be paid by the physician involved.

Claims of violation of civil rights for administration of electroconvulsive therapy over a patient's objections have not been upheld in court. In a pending case, a judge has dismissed claims of violation of civil rights in the administration of electroconvulsive therapy, over his objections and without his consent, to a patient who had been declared incompetent, on the grounds that the defendants were not acting for the state.[61] However, the case is being permitted to continue as a medical malpractice case even though consent had been given by the patient's mother, who had committed him.

Summary Comment on Right to Refuse Treatment

The posture of the courts in the cases reviewed in this section supports the idea that the right to refuse treatment is a developing doctrine. Probably more so than with any other topic discussed in this chapter, the decisions seem to reflect a move away from the therapeutic state. But perhaps a more appropriate characterization would be that a number of constraints are coming into play. Intrusive therapies will be more difficult to administer. There will be increased supervision, more review committees, and more concern with informed consent. Justification for coercive treatment will have to be put into writing on given occasions. But most of these conditions are likely to apply only to those treatments with potentially severe consequences, and there are some suggestions that "common medical practice" will be much less subject to these controls.

We should also note here the difficulty in applying the law in "total institutions" (places of residence and work cut off from the wider society). There is a tendency for inconvenient laws to be ignored and for the regulations to become an empty formality. More importantly, constitutional rights are not absolute, and in their informal operations the courts have frequently tended to conclude that forced treatment is necessary to protect families and communities.

Finally, the developing right to refuse treatment may bring to a head the conflict over involuntary commitment:

> If courts and legislators should endorse the right of patients to refuse treatment, while at the same time endorsing the concept of involuntarily committing the dangerous mentally ill, psychiatrists will find themselves acting wardens for a totally unmanageable population. If a patient refuses treatment, a psychiatrist is faced with an excruciating dilemma. If he discharges the patient, the psychiatrist may be found liable for malpractice if the patient harms himself. If he continues to retain the patient, but gives no treatment, he may be found liable as a result of the *Donaldson* decision.[62]

LEAST RESTRICTIVE ALTERNATIVE

The right to treatment in the least restrictive alternative, along with the right to refuse treatment, is one of the two major legal checks on the right to treatment.[63] The rationale for this right derives from a case unrelated to treatment in which the U.S. Supreme Court ruled that legitimate governmental purposes "cannot be pursued by means that broadly stifle fundamental personal liberties when the end can be more narrowly achieved," and promulgated the idea of "less drastic means for achieving the same basic purpose."[64] The case involved an Arkansas statute that required public school teachers to disclose the organizations to which they belonged, supposedly in the interest of occupational competence information.

The least restrictive alternative principle was first applied to civil commitment in 1966, in *Lake* v. *Cameron*.[65] This case, and *Lessard* v. *Schmidt*, established two methods of bringing alternative treatment settings to the court's attention: requiring proof of the unavailability of less restrictive alternatives by the party proposing institutionalization, or requiring the court "to examine potential treatment setting alternatives."[66]

Two cases that relate to the least restrictive alternative in therapeutic settings have been appealed to the U.S. Supreme Court. The first resulted in uncertainty in the application of the principle because the Supreme Court dismissed an appeal from the New Mexico Supreme Court, which had ruled that the state was not required to consider less restrictive alternatives to hospitalization.[67] However, this issue is also raised in *O'Connor* v. *Donaldson* in a decision that holds that involuntary commitment to custodial care will not be permissible if the person can survive outside the hospital, on his or her own or with the help of family or friends.[68] In *Donaldson*, the Supreme Court cited the case noted above, *Shelton* v. *Tucker*, when it said that incarceration is rarely necessary for merely raising the living standards of such persons otherwise capable of surviving.

Recently decided and pending court cases have applied the concept of the least restrictive alternative to institutions for the mentally ill, institutions for the mentally retarded, juvenile institutions and proceedings, and a behavior modification unit of a prison.[69]

Cases involving mental patients and the least restrictive alternative principle include two in which plaintiffs are suing for the right to be treated in the least restrictive setting.[70] One of these, *Caswell* v. *Califano*, is the first case to use only *federal* statutory and constitutional claims and the first to sue federal officials for failure to monitor adequately the state's compliance with the goals of federal acts.[71]

Other recent cases have specifically raised the issue of whether involuntary hospitalization is unconstitutional if an individual can survive outside the hospital with the help of governmental agencies, further pushing the position that involuntary hospitalization is unconstitutional if the person can survive with the help of family or friends. These cases are challenging the state's failure to create alternative treatment settings that are less restrictive than a hospital,[72] including, in some, the allocation of funds to various components of a state's mental health system.[73] In one instance, a plaintiff confined in a psychiatric ward and a nursing home is contending that he should be offered the necessary services in his own home before he is institutionalized in any way.[74] All of these cases are still pending.

Similarly, suits involving mentally retarded persons are raising the issue of whether the state can be required to create alternative treatment settings less restrictive than institutionalization. Some of these cases are seeking to require of the state specific actions that would lead to provision of less restrictive alternatives. Plaintiffs are seeking community placement of mentally retarded residents,[75] the barring of further admissions to a state institution for the mentally retarded, and the prevention of the state from constructing a new, larger, facility.[76] In the latter case, a temporary restraining order has been issued requiring the defendant to hold a public hearing on the proposed new construction before any final decision is made. A third case is more generally challenging the state's failure to provide *educational* alternatives less restrictive than institutionalization.[77] (This case illustrates again that education is sometimes legally considered a form of treatment.) All of the above cases are still pending in lower courts.

An indication of how the courts are actually ruling is provided by two recent least restrictive alternative cases concerning mentally retarded persons that have been decided by lower courts. In one, the court ordered the state to place the institutionalized plaintiff in a temporary community placement until a more permanent community placement could be found, and services appropriate for her could be developed.[78] In another, the parties had voluntarily entered into an agreement involving community-based facilities for the mentally retarded.[79] This case has been reopened, with the plaintiffs charging that the defendants have failed to implement the consent decree: the state legislature had reduced funds to the community facilities and had begun returning mentally retarded persons to the state institution. Funds have since been restored.

The issue of the least restrictive alternative has also been raised with respect to institutionalized juveniles. In one pending case, the plaintiffs are challenging the state's failure to use the least restrictive alternative in confining juveniles.[80] In another, the plaintiff is charging that the placement of status offenders with delinquent juveniles is a failure to use the least restrictive alternative.[81] In a recently decided case, the Illinois Court of Appeals did apply the doctrine of the least restrictive alternative to status offenders, specifically truant juveniles.[82] The court did not order the board of education to create new alternatives to commitment for the education of habitual truants, but it did order the board to show that "its existing less restrictive alternatives are not suitable to meet the particular needs of the habitual truant, and confinement in a parental school is a suitable means to meet those needs."

The least restrictive alternative is a relatively new legal doctrine in which details are far from having been clearly established. (It is important to note again that many of the cases described above are still in the courts.) But the outline is beginning to appear, and in a number of cases it has been held that the federal constitution requires proof that no less restrictive alternative exists prior to involuntary hospitalization.[83] It is less obvious how this principle might be applied to offenders.

What can be said at this point? Once again, the issue is not whether the state is to provide treatment for its deviants, but only the setting in which treatment is to occur. The most obvious immediate effect of the doctrine will be an expansion of therapeutic services. For example, the court's requirements in *Dixon* called for the establishment of nursing homes, personal care homes, foster homes, and halfway houses.[84] The trend seems to be to seek judicial orders that will pressure legislators and other government bodies to appropriate funds to create social systems that are not now in existence. More than any of the other legal doctrines that we have discussed, this one may succeed in getting funds transferred from institutional to community programs.

CIVIL COMMITMENT

Not surprisingly, continuing controversy surrounds the process by which the state commits individuals to mental hospitals. The surprise is that there is not more.

The anti-civil commitment human rights movement in mental health, to be sure, has enjoyed some notable, if modest success. In recent years, there has occurred an undeniable increase in awareness of the rights of patients, of legal issues in mental health, of dehumanizing institutional conditions, of the dubious efficacy of coercive treatment, and so on. The number of involuntary admissions in the United States and Canada, however, remains about as high as ever . . . . Most commitments continue to occur at present for the same reasons (e.g., "no insight") for which they have occurred for many years, despite occasional alterations in the semantic formulations of commitment statutes . . . .[85]

In spite of attempts to move towards voluntary admissions, a significant proportion of those entering mental hospitals continue to do so involuntarily (up to one-half or more in many states), with some states experiencing an increase in involuntary admissions.[86] A number of states have recently revised their mental health statutes, but not to the satisfaction of some patients. Challenges made in 1975–77 are an extension of issues that have been litigated throughout the 1970s, and the courts have responded in different ways, sometimes giving new rights to patients, while at other times simply affirming the practice that has been in existence for a number of years. There seems to be a feeling that we must circumscribe commitment powers, but there is little agreement as to how this is to be accomplished. Even the President's Commission on Mental Health was unable to recommend a single standard for all states.[87]

A majority of states have had a vague criterion for civil commitment, often couched in language such as "mentally ill and in need of care or treatment and lacks sufficient capacity to make a responsible application on his own behalf." Such a criterion was held to be constitutional by the Florida Supreme Court, but was struck down by a Pennsylvania court.[88] Several federal courts have also struck down "need-of-treatment" standards for civil commitment.[89]

During the period under review there were several state court decisions regarding the level of proof to be applied in civil commitment proceedings. On the basis of these decisions, it is not possible to come to any general conclusions regarding changes in the standards to be employed. In an April 1979 opinion, the U.S. Supreme Court ruled in Addington v. State of Texas that a "clear and convincing" standard of proof is required by the Fourteenth Amendment.[90] In choosing this intermediate standard, the Court recognized that the state could probably never prove "beyond a reasonable doubt" that an individual was mentally ill and likely to be dangerous, and that the use of such a standard may erect an immeasurable barrier to needed medical treatment. In delivering the opinion, Chief Justice Burger took note of the states' interest in providing care to citizens unable because of emotional disorder to care for themselves, and concluded that it cannot be said that it is much better for a mentally ill person to "go free" than for a mentally normal person to be committed.

A number of additional due process issues have been litigated. One state court has ruled that individuals may be held without a hearing for ten days and a second state court has approved holding an individual for twenty days without a hearing.[91] This was deemed not a denial of due process since the patient was seen as receiving treatment that might not only aid his or her mental health, but also might be necessary to an adequate and informed hearing on the necessity of commitment. Other courts have been faced with questions relating to whether an individual is entitled to trial by jury or independent psychiatric assistance at state expense;[92] a hearing before confinement;[93] and the right to competent and zealous representation in civil commitment.[94]

Within a one-year period there were at least four challenges to the authority of parents or the state to commit chidren to state mental institutions without affording them such due process protections as legal counsel and a hearing, with one of these cases resulting in a 1979 U.S. Supreme Court decision.[95] In Parham v. J.R., the Court upheld state laws that allow parents to commit minors to state mental institutions, subject to independent medical judgment.

Are there any consistent patterns to these current court cases relating to civil commitment? Yes and no. Where the question has been forcefully raised, the courts have tended to extend due process requirements with respect to hearings and legal counsel. At the same time, vague criteria for civil commitment have sometimes been affirmed and time delays have been sanctioned prior to the need for a hearing. On all of these issues there is wide variability across jurisdictions. It is still possible for a person found to be carrying $25,000 to be arrested for panhandling dimes, and involuntarily committed even with the state admitting lack of sufficient evidence to establish mental illness.[96]

The basic questions left unresolved by the Supreme Court decision in *O'Connor* v. *Donaldson* remain unresolved. And in spite of common complaints that it is "impossible" to get a person committed to a state hospital, such admissions continue at a high rate. It is true that once admitted, the length of stay has been shortened, and some people have been forced to leave the hospital against their will. A recent case seeking to enjoin a state department of mental health from *discharging* judicially committed patients from a state hospital without notice or hearing may be the first of a number to come.[97]

The results of a 1977 study in North Carolina led the investigator to sum up the problem as follows:

> Civil commitment contains inherent tensions between a benevolent ideal of treatment for the mentally ill and the harsh reality that we do so by incarcerating many against their will. This unresolved tension is manifest in our data, which show the court acting both paternalistically in following psychiatric opinion without adequate review and also "judiciously" in refusing to commit in the absence of clear, cogent, and convincing evidence of imminent danger.[98]

NOT GUILTY BY REASON OF INSANITY AND INCOMPETENCY TO STAND TRIAL

Court decisions in these two areas, which closely link the therapeutic and criminal justice systems, have not exhibited any new developments or different trends. As with other areas, there has been a tendency to ensure that all due process rights are respected in contact with the mental health system. For example, recent decisions have held that the defendant has a right to thorough testing;[99] that "extraordinary" safeguards are necessary because the conviction of an accused person who is incompetent violates due process;[100] that independent experts must be provided;[101] and that the defendant may not easily waive his or her privilege against self-incrimination.[102] This tightening of the due process requirements reflects a shift away from the therapeutic state in the sense that it invokes legal requirements rather than medical. It is not clear how much difference this emphasis of legal requirements makes in the final outcome, but it is reasonable to assume that it makes some.

Several of the recent decisions concern retarded offenders, who seem to constitute a particular problem for the courts. A defense of limited intelligence seems to be less suspect than mental illness, possibly because it is thought to be more easily identified. However, not every judge agrees about the handling of mentally retarded offenders. Following a recent decision that a defendant could not understand the significance of his guilty plea, which vacated his sentence and plea, a dissenting justice was quoted as saying "the decision licenses every illiterate moron to violate the law with impunity."[103]

A constant concern in this area relates to instances in which a defendant manufactures an insanity defense. In one such recent case, the defendant was subsequently civilly committed to a mental hospital. But he was diagnosed there as being without mental disorder, and released. The court ruled that the double jeopardy principle precluded retrying the man.[104]

Florida's recent attempt to address the manufactured defense problem through a bifurcated trial system, a provision for insanity defense proceedings only after conviction, has been ruled unconstitutional by the Florida Supreme Court.[105] The Florida court concluded that such a system raised an irrefutable presumption of intent without the prosecution having to prove intent during the conviction phase, and was thus contrary to the court's notions of due process of law. Florida thus joins Arizona, Lousiana, Texas, and Wyoming,[106] having unsuccessfully instituted bifurcated trial systems. California, Colorado, and Wisconsin have retained bifurcated systems: Colorado by determining insanity before guilt, and California and Wisconsin through doctrines of diminished responsibility whereby evidence of such nonresponsibility, but not insanity, is admissable during the intent, or conviction, phase of the trial. The weight of the bifurcated trial system trend seems to fall toward the continued therapeutic state incorporation of determinism and nonresponsibility, rather than more purely legal assumptions of free will, or choice, and responsibility.

The determination of these two issues—competency to stand trial and not guilty by reason of insanity—has continued to be a subject for heavy debate in the professional literature. But the competing perspectives have not been brought to the courts in significant numbers during the last few years, and thus it is difficult to draw conclusions regarding our major purpose of assessing the advance of the therapeutic state.

THE CONTROL OF MENTAL HEALTH
AND MEDICAL RECORDS

The kind of control that an individual has over various records relating to behavioral and medical information can serve as a further index of the growth of the therapeutic state. Concern in this area is an extension of a larger national interest in the right of privacy, an interest that has grown steadily throughout the last decade. Statements by two national commissions typify the level of concern:

> The medical-care relationship in America today is becoming dangerously fragile as the basis for the expectation of confidentiality with respect to medical records generated in that relationship is undermined more and more. A legitimate, enforceable expectation of confidentiality that will hold up under the revolutionary changes now taking place in medical care and medical recordkeeping needs to be created.[107]

> Panel members are alarmed by the extent to which requirements of informed consent for release of mental health information are ignored or abused.[108]

Since these statements were made in 1977 and 1978, a heightened sensitivity to the problem seems to have led to very little corrective action. But since voices from the political left are now being added to those from the right (who were on the scene as early as the 1950s), change is possible.

The major issue boils down to one of privacy and access to information for the individual versus the state's need to know in a variety of contexts. More specifically, controversy centers around the following issues:

1. Federal and state requirements for data about individuals for program evaluation purposes.
2. The potential loss of privacy associated with central registries involving patient identifiers.
3. The release of information to inappropriate sources—e.g., employers or collection agencies.
4. Whether in given cases more personal information is sought than is necessary to obtain objectives.
5. The extent to which the client shall have access to his or her own records, mechanisms for correcting the records, and the possibility of expungement.

This last point has received some impetus from the Privacy Act of 1974 and its "Buckley Amendment," which mandates privacy of, and access to, school records.[109] A number of model codes have been developed, and the issue of client access to records has been discussed as it applies in a variety of settings.[110]

As with several other areas discussed in this chapter, the courts are just now beginning to act on cases concerning the issues outlined above. Thus we have few recent decisions to guide us.

A person's right to privacy of medical records has been the subject of legal review in a number of recent cases. In some instances, the conflict between a state's need to have health information for purposes of employment or other reasons and the patient's right to privacy of those records has been at issue. Recent decisions involving this issue have included a Blue Cross agreement, under threat of suit, to delete three questions involving degree of impairment from a mental health report form it was using with federal employees in the Washington, D.C. area.[111] There was concern that such information could prejudice the careers of those seeking treatment, and discourage federal employees from seeking treatment. A second instance, not yet before a court, challenges a standard question asked by the New Jersey bar's committee on character, regarding whether the applicant to the bar had ever been treated for any mental disorder.[112] A third instance, which is before a court, challenges a county government's right to ask job applicants questions about health and to obtain both physical and mental health records. The issues include whether disclosure of the information is necessary and relevant to a person's ability to perform a job, and whether the county government has effective safeguards against improper use or dissemination of the information.[113] A related case challenged the central computerization of mental health records by the New York State Department of Mental Hygiene.[114] The challenge was denied by the lower court and the New York Court of Appeals.

The question of access to records has been at issue, both in cases where records have been withheld from parents or others needing them for investigation and in cases where records have been released to persons whose right to receive them has been challenged. A district court in Pennsylvania has protected plaintiff's attorneys' right of access to medical records in a case involving conditions at an institution for the mentally retarded.[115] A Delaware court has also upheld the right of an attorney and parents to a learning-disabled child's records in a case challenging the school placement of the child.[116] In two other cases involving investigation of conditions, the issue is the right of investigators to records that are not exclusively medical. In one case, plaintiffs are challenging the denial of records of an incident concluding in the suicide of a psychiatric patient allegedly homosexually abused by a staff member.[117] In another instance, a New York district court has ordered a youth camp's officials to allow a team of mental health professionals access to records, inmates, and staff. The suit is seeking to prevent the state of New York from forcing youths confined in the camp to perform work without pay.[118]

Recent cases have challenged the access to medical and mental health records by unauthorized persons. *Whelan* v. *Roe*, involving the confidentiality of drug prescriptions, was heard by the U.S. Supreme Court.[119] Another case before the California Superior Court challenges the release of confidential patient records to private collection agencies for collection of delinquent accounts.[120]

Suit has been brought for the expungement of hospital records on people illegally committed[121] or observed but released.[122] Both of these are pending.

The above cases reflect an increased concern about protecting patient records while simultaneously giving the patient access to them. Whether this heightened sensitivity gets translated into day-to-day operations of the institutions concerned remains an open question.

RIGHT TO EDUCATION

The legal concept of the right to education is related to the more general concept of the therapeutic state, even though traditional medical professionals are not directly involved. One link is contextual; as noted earlier, the right to education is frequently introduced in connection with the right to treatment. The second link concerns the type of people for whom the right to education is requested. These usually include those who otherwise would be in treatment with a therapeutic professional, e.g., the mentally retarded or delinquent who are usually included in the larger class of handicapped or developmentally disabled children.

The issues addressed by the courts under the concept of the right to education include the right of developmentally disabled children to a free public education; the procedures and rights involved in classification of developmentally disabled children for educational purposes; the right of institutionalized children, both the developmentally disabled and the delinquent, to education; the circumstances and procedures under which a school may exclude a child; and implemental questions such as the setting of deadlines, and the failure of a state legislature to appropriate adequate funds to carry out the court's requirements. The latter issue raises the question of federalism—the authority of a federal court to make requirements that may infringe on the authority of the state.

The arguments used in these cases are based on the Education for All Handicapped Children Act; the Rehabilitation Act of 1973; various state statutes regarding education of the handicapped; federal and/or state constitutional guarantees of equal protection; and *Brown* v. *Board of Education,* which decided that when a state provides an opportunity for education, it must be available to all on equal terms.[123]

A large number of recent cases have addressed the right of developmentally disabled children to a publicly funded education. The first ruling under the Education for All Handicapped Children Act came from a Mississippi district court, *Mattie T.* v. *Holladay.*[124] This case established that an individual has a federal cause of action under the act, and that state departments of education have the responsibility to enforce the act. The plaintiffs, handicapped children, had charged that the Mississippi Department of Education had violated their rights under the act in a number of ways, including failure to provide a program to locate and identify handicapped children in the state in need of special educational services, and failure to provide to the maximum extent possible educational programs in normal school settings with nonhandicapped children.

Courts in a number of additional cases have ruled that states must provide public education for all handicapped children.[125] One pending case is challenging both unnecessary segregation of handicapped children and their placement in a regular school environment without supplementary services.[126] That the state not only must provide appropriate educational services for all disabled children, but must also make them available without cost to parents, has been ruled in a number of instances.[127] The pending cases of *Crowder* v. *Riles* and *Sussan* v. *East Brunswick Board of Education, et al.* are seeking this same requirement.[128]

Not unexpectedly, since courts repeatedly have been asked to settle the issue of whether free public education is a right of disabled children, they have also been asked to address the issue of when children may be excluded from public education, including both the condition of the child that would warrant exclusion, and the rights that exist for children in expulsion and suspension procedures.

A Pennsylvania district court has been asked to determine whether the rights in expulsion and suspension proceedings extended to mentally retarded children apply to emotionally disturbed and learning-disabled children.[129] In Minnesota, a district court awarded compensatory damages to an emotionally handicapped child who was dismissed from school for hitting a teacher. The court ruled that the violation was not willful, and that the plaintiff's rights had been violated when dismissed.[130] A similar case involved a child with emotional, social, and mental handicaps who had been permanently expelled from a public special education class for attempting to start a fight with another child. Five months later the state began providing three hours per week instruction for him at home, a program that the complainant claimed was inadequate and inappropriate. By consent decree, the state agreed to provide educational services in the public school to the greatest extent possible. Compensatory and punitive damages are pending.[131]

Concerning conditions of the child that warrant exclusion from public education, an Ohio district court ruled in 1976 that exclusion from school of children who have been found incapable of profiting substantially by further instruction does not violate the equal protection clause.[132]

The related issue of the right of institutionalized children to education has also been addressed by the courts. A New Jersey court has been asked to rule on the adequacy of the educational and training program at an institute for the mentally retarded.[133] Included in the charges is the institute's failure to develop meaningful individualized educational plans. In two other pending cases, the plaintiffs, residents in juvenile detention centers, are arguing for their right to education.[134] In one of these, an attempt is being made to link the right to education with the right to treatment; the residents are arguing that the right to education is an indispensable element of the right to treatment for juveniles.[135]

Testing and classification is yet another issue related to the right to education of developmentally disabled children with which courts have become involved. The significant *Mattie T. v. Holladay* case addressed several issues of classification. The plaintiff in that case, handicapped children, won:

1. Procedural safeguards to challenge decisions on educational evaluation and placement, including prior notice and an impartial due process hearing;
2. The establishment of a program to identify all handicapped children in the state in need of special educational classes;
3. Classification by racially and culturally nondiscriminatory tests and procedures.

Courts have also dealt with the issue of the right to evaluation and classification[136] and the issue of due process in testing and evaluation.[137] The rulings in all four of these cases were consistent with those of the *Mattie T. v. Holladay* ruling.

Implementation of the court decisions has been approached in a number of ways. In the *Mattie T. v. Holladay* case, the judge set deadlines by which certain segments of the decision had to be implemented. This is considered significant in that it established the right of developmentally disabled children to immediate services, even though not all plaintiffs had been excluded totally from educational services. Some had been in regular classes; others were in inadequate special classes. In the *Allen* v. *McDonough* case, the judge also imposed a deadline, then held the school committee members and the school superintendent in contempt for not meeting the deadline.

One court case was a major factor in the passage of a state law on education of the handicapped, the Colorado Handicapped Children's Educational Act.[138] The court initially rejected attempts to dismiss, after enactment of the law, stating that "mere enactment without implementation" would not satisfy the plaintiffs' claims. A voluntary move by the plaintiffs to dismiss was later granted.

Difficulty in implementing court decisions is illustrated in the *Mills* v. *Board of Education of District of Columbia* case, settled in 1972. Despite returns to court and contempt proceedings against the defendants, the court orders have not been implemented. A detailed plan for suitable public education of developmentally disabled children, ordered by the court, has not yet been developed, and many institutionalized juvenile and mentally retarded children still do not have access to educational services.[139]

The issue of federalism arose in the *Rainey* v. *Tennessee Department of Education* case, in which attempts by the court to implement previous court orders, a consent decree, and a state law requiring special education for handicapped children led to challenges on the ground of separation of powers and sovereign immunity. The court had imposed a deadline for implementation and enjoined the state from expending funds for the operation of the public school system if the deadline was not met. The defendants claimed they could not implement the consent decree because the legislature had failed to increase funding. The court held that the consent decree did not require extra money; if a state has a free public school system, it cannot discriminate against a small minority.[140]

Yet another approach to encouraging the establishment of special education programs, and screening and evaluation, occurred in *Pierce* v. *Board of Education of the City of Chicago*.[141] In this case, the court ruled that a learning-disabled student could maintain a damage action against the board of education for emotional and psychic injury alleged to have been caused by the board's failure to transfer the student from regular to special education classes. (The transfer had been advised both by the parents and a private physician.) The court ruled that the board's failure to evaluate or transfer the student or to notify the superintendent could amount to intentional breach of duty.

The above review reflects considerable judicial activity regarding the right to education for handicapped children. On the whole, the court rulings seem to reflect an awareness that historically, mentally handicapped children have been excluded from a free public education and that this exclusion violates the equal protection and due process clauses of the Constitution. In the same sense that a trend exists to require individual treatment plans for mental patients, there is a parallel trend to require individualized educational plans. Such plans are likely to require the employment of additional therapeutic staff, including psychologists, teachers, physical therapists, etc.

On the whole, there is probably less ideological conflict and controversy in this area than in any other reviewed in this chapter. The problems that do exist concern the availability of funds (and priorities), and questions about the appropriateness of federal intervention. The problems of implementation noted so many times before also prevail here.

GUARDIANSHIP AND CONSERVATORSHIP

Recent issues in the conservatorship-guardianship area have included the constitutionality of the state's acting as conservator for institutionalized persons, the procedural due process of state conservatorship, and procedures involved in assigning guardians for adult converts to religions that are seen as unacceptable by the parents of the converts.

Courts in two recent cases have found unconstitutional state conservatorships of the assets of institutionalized mentally ill and mentally retarded persons. A federal district court in Connecticut has ruled unconstitutional the seizure of funds by the state, acting as conservator, from institutionalized mentally retarded and mentally ill persons whose assets did not exceed $5,000.[142] The court enjoined the state from accepting additional funds, but held that it lacked jurisdiction under the Eleventh Amendment to compel the court to return the unconstitutionally seized funds. In 1974, a three-judge court ruled that the Pennsylvania statutes permitting the summary appropriation and control of mental patients' funds were unconstitutional. For the next nine months, the state continued to withhold patients' funds. Plaintiffs filed a motion for contempt, which resulted in a court order to return nine million dollars. An appeal to the Third Circuit was denied. Further application was made to the U.S. Court of Appeals, and a partial stay of the order to return the funds was granted.[143]

Two pending cases are challenging state conservatorship statues on procedural due process grounds. Both involve conservatorship for estates of institutionalized persons.[144]

In a related area, guardianship, at least three cases are pending that involve parental guardianship of adult converts to the Hare Krishna religion.[145] In one of these, *Bavis* v. *McKenna,* a federal damages action has been filed against a judge, a lawyer, and a deprogramming team. This is the first suit to seek damages from a judge for issuing a secret *ex parte* order finding a person mentally incompetent without psychiatric testimony and without due process. The plaintiff was without forcibly confined in a hotel room for four days, then taken to a deprogramming center. Feigning renunciation of her beliefs, she was released, dissolved the guardianship, and returned to the Hare Krishna temple.

MISCELLANEOUS CASES

Under this heading we will discuss briefly a number of disparate cases that do not fit into the preceding major categories, but which do relate to the basic questions regarding the therapeutic state.

The extent to which specific sexual behavior concerns issues of sin or sickness was a consideration in several court decisions. In one such decision, the court affirmed the role of psychiatry in dealing with homosexuality.[146] A teacher's support of gay rights was interpreted by two psychiatrists as deviation from normal health; in view of this finding, the requirement of the board of education that the teacher subject himself to a psychiatric exam was found to be fair and reasonable. In a similar situation in Washington, the school board was more straightforward in firing an avowed homosexual because his sexual preference constituted immorality.[147]

The need for treatment for disordered sex offenders was made clear in a court finding that holding such a person, without treatment, in institutional units in penal settings that were in reality prisons, amounted to cruel and unusual punishment.[148] In this particular case, the court tightened the standard of evidence required in sex offender proceedings from the preponderance of the evidence to that of beyond a reasonable doubt.

Within the last two years there have been at least three rulings on eligibility for public benefits for transsexual surgery. In two of these cases the court held that the individuals were eligible for benefits and that there could be no discrimination on the basis of diagnosis or illness.[149] In the third case, the court found that there was no requirement to finance every health care service deemed beneficial.[150]

The question of sickness versus responsibility was an issue in two other cases involving benefits. In one instance, it was determined that a manic-depressive who resigned from his job during a manic state qualified for unemployment benefits.[151] In a case yet to be decided, a petitioner discharged from his job for a five-day absence because he was drinking was denied unemployment compensation because he was fired for cause. He claimed that alcoholism is a disease, and that he lost the job because of the disease and not misconduct. Consequently, he claimed eligibility for compensation.[152]

It is now well established that the courts view alcoholism primarily as a sickness, and the cases that we found during this period support this interpretation. A California judge ruled that it is an unconstitutional imposition of cruel and unusual punishment to jail and convict a person who can successfully plead that he suffers from alcoholism to the point where he cannot take care of himself and cannot refrain from drinking in public.[153]

In a case difficult to classify, a bearded man dressed in women's clothing was taken to Bellevue as a "dangerously mentally ill person." He claimed that he was trying to make a political statement regarding women's role in society, and gained his freedom. He seeks damages for the arrest.[154]

There has been continuing debate regarding the right to remain silent during attempted diagnostic exams. According to a Maryland Court of Appeals, individuals referred to Patuxent Institution for an examination must cooperate with the medical staff making the examination.[155] It was ruled that the Fifth Amendment privilege against self-incrimination was not applicable to the defective delinquent statute and that individuals failing to cooperate could be held indefinitely.

Finally, we consider two cases involving sterilization laws, long considered the ultimate expression of the therapeutic state. In one such case a federal court overruled a district court that had dismissed a case against a judge who had ordered the sterilization of a fifteen-year-old girl, with the finding that he had not provided due process on a number of counts.[156] Another three-judge federal court upheld the constitutionality of almost all of North Carolina's new sterilization statutes. The North Carolina statute states that it is the *duty* of the director of an institution or the director of county social services to institute sterilization procedures under specific circumstances.[157] This would include situations in which it is considered to be in the best interests of the person or the public, or both, and when the retarded person is judged likely to procreate a defective child, or would be unable to care for the child.

RESPONSIBILITY OF THE THERAPIST

A somewhat crude but not unreasonable index of the advancement of the therapeutic state is the extent to which various therapists are held responsible for the behavior of their clients or patients. If the therapist is liable, then the patient must be sick and not responsible. An analysis of court decisions on this topic could also provide some insight on what mental health professionals can reasonably be expected to do in light of current knowledge.

Physicians have been required for a number of years to exercise a social control function in reporting such things as gunshot wounds and suicide attempts. Under one court decision they could now be held liable for injuries induced by a third person. This would occur in a situation where a physician failed to diagnose and report child abuse, and the child was later injured.[158] This principle was extended in the well-known Tarasoff decision, a situation involving a patient telling his therapist about intentions to harm a girlfriend, intentions that were later acted on.[159] It was held that the therapist was responsible for failing to warn the third party. The implications of this decision are still being discussed widely, and with considerable alarm, among professional associations. It is interesting to note that the suit elicited detailed statements from professional groups acknowledging the difficulties in attempting to predict dangerous behavior—something that some of these same professionals had been doing in the courtrooms on a daily basis.

The cause for concern is understandable, since various court decisions imply that the ability to predict future dangerousness must exist. In this regard, the failure to make such predictions has resulted in the extension of liability to individuals as well as institutions. For example, a U.S. Court of Appeals has ruled that a psychiatrist, a private psychiatric institution, and a probation officer must pay $25,000 to the mother of a young woman slain by a released mental patient.[160] There is a case pending in Massachusetts in which a patient hanged herself while in the hospital; her husband has charged that the superintendent failed to exercise necessary precautions.[161]

Those alarmed by this trend may take some comfort in two decisions in which authorities were found not to be responsible for acts committed by released patients. But an examination of the details in these cases would limit the amount of comfort derived: in one situaion the violent act occurred two years after release from the hospital,[162] and in the other the victim was found to have played an instigating role.[163]

The courts have continued to award damages against individual staff members for inappropriate management and treatment of hospitalized mental patients, and such cases continue to be filed.[164] *O'Connor* v. *Donaldson,* upheld by the U.S. Supreme Court in 1975, is probably the best known of these.[165] The kinds of issues being litigated are well illustrated in a major trial that began in Boston in December, 1977, in which a number of patients are suing fifteen of their former doctors at Boston State Hospital.[166] The patients seek over a million dollars in damages on the grounds that they were improperly secluded and improperly medicated. The extreme to which the responsibility question may be carried was seen in an unsuccessful case brought by a Florida mental patient. The patient sued the state for damages on the grounds that they had inappropriately released him, leading to suffering on his part as a result of his having killed a man while out of the hospital.

In summary, although some of the cases reviewed here have been primarily concerned with protecting constitutional rights, the net effect of these and related decisions has been to extend both the responsibilities of the treating agent and the general assumption that the state in its various forms has a responsibility for the welfare and protection of its charges.

OVERVIEW

As indicated at the beginning of this chapter, our interest was the relatively modest one of evaluating current court cases according to how much they affirm or deny the advancement of the therapeutic state. It seems clear to us that the courts, with very few exceptions, support the notion that the state has a very direct and continuing responsibility to provide therapeutic services to an ever larger number of its citizens, without regard to setting or type of institution. The current skepticism concerning the failures of rehabilitation seems generally not to have reached the courts, or if it has, the impact has been minimized. Rehabilitative services are being required on both constitutional and statutory grounds, under the exercise of police and *parens patriae* powers.

This general trend to expand therapeutic services has been accompanied by an affirmation of individual rights—the right to refuse treatment, the application of full due process, attempts to tighten the criteria for civil commitment, and the like. But with respect to the larger question being posed in this paper, it should be recognized that these rights relate primarily to the question of *how* and *where* the services are to be rendered, not whether they are to be provided in the first place. The role of mental health professionals in addressing troublesome behavior has been affirmed time and time again.

While there is professional concern about ethical problems for mental health professionals in the exercise of coercive powers, our impression is that alarm over the growth of the therapeutic state is on the wane.

National figures who have previously expressed concern over the abuses of psychiatric power now seem to feel that this concern is misplaced.[167] Increasingly, complaints are heard about the "roadblocks" to treatment thrown up by those pushing for further legal protections. Most of this alarm comes from people who have a strong faith in the reliability of psychiatric classification and in the effectiveness of treatment, a faith not shared by all of those intimate with the workings of the therapeutic state.

Whether or not it is considered desirable, there is no question that the courts continue to be drawn into the delivery of therapeutic services, and that they are playing an increasingly active role. In a recent law review article, Abram Chayes has summarized this trend and called attention to the shift in judicial role.[168] Time after time, judges have played factfinding and administrative roles through jurisdiction retained in complicated cases. They have spelled out specific treatment standards in great detail and they have been directly involved in the delivery of services. The legal and treatment systems particularly are being brought into continuous mutual involvement through the use of standing panels of experts.

One result of this trend to judicial involvement in administrative decisionmaking has been reduction of the powers of administrators and a strengthening of the rights of the receivers of service.[169] Reasonable people will differ as to whether this constitutes a step forward or a step backward. The degree of alarm one experiences is correlated with the perceived impact of court decisions. There can be no question that in some instances court decisions have resulted in large increases in budgets for various state institutions, but for the most part, reserve regarding the degree of change that has occurred would seem to be in order.

There is by now a widespread understanding that social change is slow in coming. Specifically, in the mental health field there is no trouble at all in pointing to case after case where court decisions have been ignored. The U.S. Supreme Court ruling in *Donaldson* has not been implemented to any significant extent. Involuntary admissions to state mental hospitals continue much as in the past despite statutory changes and court rulings. Further relief is being sought in *Wyatt* v. *Stickney* eight years after the court order.[170] And so on. Time after time the courts have had to resort to contempt citations and threats in order to move anything at all. (It is at least in part this failure to respond that has brought the courts into the administrative and decisionmaking role.)

There is good reason to believe that contact between the criminal justice and mental health systems will continue to expand, and that the mental health system will be even more directly involved in providing services under varying degrees of coercion. Thus we would argue that concerns about the therapeutic state expressed eight to ten years ago are even more valid today.

NOTES

1. Ennis, B. J. Judicial involvement in the public practice of psychiatry. In W. E. Barton and C. J. Sanborn (Eds.), *Law and the Mental Health Professions,* International Universities Press, 1978, p. 5.
2. Ibid., p. 6.
3. Washington v. United States, 390 F.2d 444 (D.C. Cir. 1967).
4. Id. n.33. See also People v. Fuller, 24 N.Y. 2d 292 (1968) (concern about the law adopting the "medical model" in expert witness situation).
5. Millard v. Harris, 406 F.2d 964 (D.C. Cir. 1968).
6. Ibid.
7. Durham v. United States, 214 F.2d 862 (D.C. Cir. 1954).
8. McDonald v. United States, 312 F.2d 847 (D.C. Cir. 1962).
9. United States v. Eichberg, 439 F.2d 620 nn.30 & 31 (D.C. Cir. 1970); United States v. Alexander, 471 F.2d 923 nn.117 & 121 (D.C. Cir. 1970); United States v. Brawner, 471 F.2d 969 (D.C. Cir. 1972); Hartwell v. United States 353 F. Supp. 354 n.15 (D.D.C. 1972); United States v. Moore, 486 F.2d 1139 nn.99 & 100 (D.C. Cir. 1973).
10. See Arthurs v. Regan, 69 Misc. 2d 363 (N.Y. Sup. Ct. 1972) ("medical model of not sharing diagnoses with patients is breaking down"); Commonwealth v. Jarvis, Mass. App. Ct. Adv. Sh. 193 (Worcester App. Ct. of Mass. 1974) (citing Dershowitz re "medical model").
11. Suzuki v. Quisenberry, 411 F. Supp. 1113 (D. Hawaii 1976) (in the summary).
12. Ibid. (in the synopsis).
13. Ibid.
14. Crouse & McGinnis v. Murray, No. 575-191 (N.D. Ind., filed Nov. 17, 1975); Davis v. Balson, No. C73-205 (N.D. Ohio, Jan. 21, 1977); Doe v. Hudspeth, No. J75-36(c) (S.D. Miss., Feb. 17, 1977); Halderman & United States v. Pennhurst, C.A. No. 74-1345 (E.D. Pa. Nov. 30, 1976); Horack v. Exon, No. 72-L-299 (D. Neb. 1973); Navarro v. Hernandez, No.74-1301 (D.P.R. Apr. 20, 1977); NYSARC & Parisi v. Carey, 393 F. Supp. 715 (E.D. N.Y. 1975), 357 F. Supp. 752 (E.D. N.Y. 1973); Ohio Association for Retarded Citizens v. Moritz, No. C2-76-398 (S.D. Ohio, Apr. 19, 1977); Patients v. Camden County Board of Chosen Freeholders, No. L-33417-74-P.W. (N.J. Sup. Ct. Camden Co., filed Apr. 29, 1977); Santana v. Rios, No. 75-1187 (D.P.R., filed Oct. 17, 1975); Schindenwolf v. Klein, No. A-2695-76 (N.J. Sup. Ct. App. Div., filed July 27, 1977); Wuori v. Bruns, No. 75-80 (D. Me., filed Oct. 1, 1975); Wyatt v. Stickney, 344 F. Supp. 373, 387 (M.D. Ala. 1972), aff'd 503 F.2d 1305 (5th Cir. 1974).
15. NYSARC and Parisi v. Carey, 393 F. Supp. 715 (E.D. N.Y. 1975), 357 F. Supp. 752 (E.D. N.Y. 1973).
16. Patients v. Camden County Board of Chosen Freeholders, No. L-33417-74-P.W. (N.J. Sup. Ct. Camden Co., filed Apr. 29, 1977).
17. State v. Alton, 362 A.2d 545 (N.J., 1976).
18. Davis V. Balson, No. C73-205 (N.D. Ohio, 1977); NYSARC and Parisi v. Carey, 393 F. Supp. 715 (E.D. N.Y. 1975), 357 F. Supp. 752 (E.D. N.Y. 1973); Welsch v. Likins, 373 F. Supp. 487 (D. Minn. 1974).
19. Vanderzeil v. Hudspeth, Civ. Act. No. J76-262R (S.D. Miss. 1977).
20. Testimony before U.S. Senate Subcommittee, quoted in *Behavior Today,* 1977, 4-5, October 31.
21. President's Commission on Mental Health. Vol IV, Report of the Task Panel on Legal and Ethical Issues. U.S. Government Printing Office, 1978, p. 1455.
22. Bresolin v. Morris, 558 P.2d 1350 (Wash. 1977).
23. Bowring v. Godwin, 551 F.2d 44 (C.A. Va. 1977).
24. In re D.F., A-1620-75 (N.J. Super. Ct. 1976).

25. Pugh v. Locke, 406 F. Supp. 318, (M.D. Ala. 1976).
26. White v. Morris, No. 67488/68250/789666 (Wash. Sup. Ct., King County, 1975).
27. James v. Wallace, 406 F. Supp. 318 (M.D. Ala. 1976); Laaman v. Helgemoe, 437 F. Supp. 269 (D.N.H. 1977).
28. Sandoval v. Noren, C-72-2213-RFP/SJ (N.D. Cal. 1976).
29. Jackson v. McLemore, 523 F.2d 838 (8th Cir. 1975).
30. Bowen v. Werner, 75-482 (E.D. Pa. 1976); Doe v. Holladay, No. CU-77-74 BLG (D. Mont., filed May 24, 1977).
31. Morgan v. Sproat, No. J75-21(0) (S.D. Miss. 1977).
32. Bowring, supra Note 23.
33. Montana v. Clark, No. 4238 (Mont. Dist. Ct., Lewis & Clark Co., July 15, 1977).
34. President's Commission on Mental Health, Vol. IV, Report, p. 1456.
35. Ibid.
36. Sites v. McKenzie, 76-24-W (N.D. W. Va. 1976).
37. Cruz v. Ward, No. 77-7043 (2d Cir. 1977).
38. Kassirer, L.B. The right to treatment and the right to refuse treatment. *Journal of Psychiatry and Law*, 1974, 2, p. 461.
39. Ibid., p. 462.
40. Plotkin, R. Limiting the therapeutic orgy: mental patients' right to refuse treatment. *Northwestern University Law Review*, 1977, 72, pp. 490–491.
41. Ibid., pp. 493–497.
42. Price v. Sheppard, 239 N.W. 2d 905 (Minn. Sup. Ct. 1976).
43. In re the Alleged Mental Illness of Paul Fussa, No. 46912 (Minn. Sup. Ct. 1976).
44. Doe v. Klein, No. L-12088-74 P.W. (N.J. Super. Ct. 1977). Wyatt v. Stickney, No. 344 F. Supp. 373, 387 (M.D. Ala. 1972), aff'd 503 F.2d 1305 (5th Cir. 1974).
45. Wyatt v. Stickney, No. 344 F. Supp, 373, 387 (M.D. Ala. 1972), aff'd 503 F.2d 1305 (5th Cir. 1974).
46. Kaimowitz v. Department of Mental Health, No. 73-19434 (AWC Cir. Ct., Wayne Co., Mich., 1973).
47. Scott v. Plante, 532 F.2d (3d Cir 1976); Souder v. McGuire, 423 F. Supp. 830, 832 (M.D. Pa. 1976); Levine v. Zitway, Civil Docket #77-104 SD, J.S. District Court for the District of Maine.
48. Winters v. Miller, No. 466 F.2d 65 (3d Cir. 1971).
49. Matukia v. Beal, No. 77-0000 (W.D. Pa., filed Jan. 3, 1977).
50. Souder v. McGruie, No. 74-590 (M.D. Pa. 1976).
51. Jackson v. Indiana, 406 U.S. 715 (1972).
52. Nelson v. Heyne, No. 491 F.2d 352 (7th Cir. Ct. 1974).
53. Okin v. Rogers, No. 77-1201 (1st Cir. Ct. App., filed Mar. 29, 1977).
54. Liles v. Ward, N. 76-Civ.-4786 (S.D. N.Y. 1976).
55. Knecht v. Gillman, 488 F.2d 1136 (8th Cir. Ct. 1973).
56. In re Hospitalization of C.B., No. AM-774-75 (N.J. Super. Ct., Mercer Co., App. Div., filed Aug. 2, 1976).
57. Jones v. Saikewicz, No. 711 (Mass. Sup. Jud. Ct. 1976).
58. Nelson v. Hudspeth, No. GC74-1005 (N.D. Miss. 1977).
59. Rogers v. Macht, Civ. No. 75-1610T (D. Mass. 1977).
60. Pettis v. State Department of Hospitals, 336 So.2d 521 (La. App., 1976).
61. Risley v. Coombs, No. N-76-234 (Fed. Ct., filed Feb. 17, 1976).
62. Kapolow, L.E. Patients' rights and psychiatric practice. In W. E. Barton and C. J. Sanborn (Eds.), *Law and the Mental Health Professions*. International Universities Press, 1978, 264-265.
63. National Association of Attorneys General, Committee on the Office of Attorney

General, *The Right to Treatment in Mental Health Law* 46 (February 1976).

64. Shelton v. Tucker, 364 U.S. 479 (1960).
65. Lake v. Cameron, 364 F. 2d 657 (D.C. Cir. 1966).
66. Lessard v. Schmidt, 349 F. Supp. 1078 (E.D. Wis. 1972), *remanded for classification*, 414 U.S. 473 (1974), as reported in National Association of Attorneys General, supra note 63, at 53.
67. State v. Sanchez, 80 N.M. 439, 457 P.2d 370 (1969), *appeal dismissed*, 396 U.S. 276 (1970).
68. O'Connor v. Donaldson, 422 U.S. 563 (1975).
69. Bowen v. Werner, No. 75–482 (E.D. Pa. 1976).
70. Caswell v. Califano, No. 77–0488 CU–W–4 (W.D. Mo., filed June 30, 1977).
71. *Clearinghouse Review* 504, September 1977.
72. Doe v. Yuen, Civ. No. 77–0059 (D. Hawaii, filed Feb. 23, 1977; Dixon v. Weinberger, 405 F. Supp. 974 (D.D.C. 1975).
73. Brewster v. Dukakis, No. 76–4423–F (D. Mass., filed Mar. 15, 1977).
74. McNairy v. Altman, No. 77–3112 DWW (C.D. Cal., filed Aug. 18, 1977).
75. Bettencourt v. Rhodes, No. C77–12 (N.C. Ohio, filed Jan. 12, 1977).
76. Kentucky Association for Retarded Citizens v. Connecticut, No. C–77–0048P (W.D. Ky., filed June 2, 1977), as reported in 2 *Amicus* 23 (November 1977).
77. New Jersey Association for Retarded Citizens v. New Jersey Department of Human Services, No. C2473–76 (Super. Ct., Hunterdon Cty., N.J., filed Mar. 16, 1977).
78. In re Deborah P., No. 76–26504 (P. Div. Pickaway Cty., Ohio, 1977).
79. Horacek v. Exon, No. 72–L–299, 357 F. Supp. 71 (D. Neb. 1973).
80. Santiago v. Philadelphia, No. 74–2589 (E.D. Pa. 1977).
81. Benitez v. Collazo, No. 77–662 (D.P.R., filed May 2, 1977).
82. Chicago Board of Education v. Terrile, 47 Ill. App. 3d 75 (Ill. Ct. App., 1977).
83. President's Commission on Mental Health, Vol. IV, Report, p. 1428.
84. Dixon v. Weinberger, 405 F. Supp. 974 (D.D.C. 1975).
85. Page, S. Power, professionals, and arguments against civil commitment. *Professional Psychology*, 1975, 6, p. 387.
86. For example, involuntary patients in the Texas system increased from 8,600 in 1975 to 9,200 in 1977. *Wall Street Journal*, Jan. 24, 1978, p. 1.
87. President's Commission on Mental Health, Vol. IV, Report, p. 1445.
88. In re Beverly, 342 So.2d 481 (Fla. 1977); Commonwealth ex rel Fenkin v. Roop, 339 A.2d 764 (Pa. 1975).
89. Doremus v. Farrell, 407 F. Supp. 509,514 (D. Neb. 1975); Kendall v. True, 391 F. Supp. 413 (W.D. Ky. 1975); Lynch v. Baxley, 386 F. Supp. 378 (M.D. Ala. 1974); Bell v. Wayne County General Hospital, 384 F. Supp. 1085 (E.D. Mich. 1974); Lessard v. Schmidt, 349 F. Supp. 1078 (E.D. Wis. 1972), *vacated*, 414 U.S. 473 (1974), *on remand*, 379 F. Supp. 1376 (E.D., Wis. 1974), *vacated*, 421 U.S. 957 (1975), *on remand*, 413 F. Supp 1318 (E.D. Wis. 1976).
90. Addington v. Texas, 99 S. Ct. 1804 (1979).
91. Call v. Hyland, 411 F. Supp. 905 (D.N.J. 1976); French v. Blackburn, No. C–76–52–WS (M.D. N.C. 1977).
92. Dorsey v. Solomon, No. H–75–1406 (D. Md. 1977).
93. In re Tules, 6116 (Nev. Dist. Ct., Washoe Co., 1977).
94. Memmel v. Mundy, No. 76–170 (Wis. Sup. Ct. 1977).
95. In re Rogers, S. Crim. No. 19558 (Cal. Sup. Ct. 1977); Johnson v. Solomon, (D. Md., filed Dec. 10, 1976); Kremens v. Bartley, No. 75–1064 (U.S. Sup. Ct. 1977); Parham v. J.R., 99 S. Ct. 2493 (1979).
96. Friedman v. Escalona, No. 75 C4414, (N.D. 471, filed Dec. 30, 1975).

97. Hildenbrand v. Smith, 770399 (E.D. Mich., filed Feb.17, 1977).

98. Hiday, V. A. Reformed commitment procedures: an empirical study in the courtroom. *Law & Society Review* 1977, 11, p. 665.

99. Louisiana v. Bennett, 58 536 (La. Sup. Ct. 1977).

100. United States v. Masthers, No. 74-1602 (U.S. App. D.C. 1976).

101. In re Whitehouse, 56 Ill. App. 3d 245 (Ill. App. Ct., filed 1977).

102. People v. Parker, 119 Cal. Rptr. 49, Cal. App. (1975).

103. Supra note 96.

104. United States v. Carter, 415 F. Supp. 15 (D.D.C. 1975).

105. State ex rel. Boyd v. Green, 52 678 (Fla. Sup. Ct. 1978).

106. Sanchez v. State, 567 P.2d 270 (Wyo. 1977).

107. Privacy Protection Study Commission, *Personal Privacy in an Information Society*, 1977, p. 306.

108. President's Commission on Mental Health, Vol. IV, Report, p. 1401.

109. Privacy Act of 1974, U.S.C. 522a; The Family Educational Rights and Privacy Act, 20 U.S.C. 1232g.

110. Fischer, C. T., and Brodsky, S. L. *Client Participation in Human Services.* Transaction Books, 1978.

111. *Intrusive Questions Removed from Blue Cross Report Forms* 3 *Mental Health Law Project Summary of Activities* 1–2 (Summer 1977).

112. In re Jean Ross, as reported in 2 *Mental Health Law Project Summary of Activities* 5 (Fall 1976).

113. Womeldorf v. Gleason, Civ. Act. B-75-1086 (D.C. Md., filed Aug. 6, 1975).

114. Volkman v. Miller, 383 N.Y.S.2d (Sup. Ct. 1976).

115. Bartley v. Kremens, 402 F. Supp. 1039 (E.D. Pa. 1975), *remanded* 97 S. Ct. 1709 (1977).

116. Kiliany v. Vaul, No. 76-3220 (Pa. C.P., Delaware Co., filed Mar. 15, 1976).

117. Board of Visitors v. Bronx Psychiatric Center, M.H.L.P.H. (3) (Fall, 1976).

118. King v. Carey, No. 75-14 (JTC) (W.D. N.Y. 1977).

119. Whelan v. Roe, 403 F. Supp. 931 (96 S. Ct. 1100 1976).

120. Roe v. Peninsula Hosp., No. 208797 (Cal. Super. Ct., San Mateo Co., filed Jan. 27, 1977).

121. Wolfe v. Beale, 376 (Sup. Ct., E.D. Pa. 1976).

122. Chico v. New York City Transit Authority, No. 21366 (N.Y.S. Sup. Ct., filed Dec. 3, 1975).

123. Education of the Handicapped Act, 20 U.S. C.§§1401 et seq.; Brown v. Board of Education, 347 U.S. 483 (1954).

124. Mattie T. v. Holladay, No. DC75-31-5 (N.D. Miss. 1977).

125. Allen v. McDonough, No. 14948 (Mass. Super. Ct., Suffolk Co., 1976); Colorado Association for Retarded Citizens v. State Department of Education No. C-4620 (D. Col.) as reported in *Mental Retardation and the Law* 3 (December 1975); Cook v. Edwards, No. 341 F. Supp. 307 (D.N.H. 1972); Fialkowski v. Shapp, 405 F. Supp. 946 (E.D. Pa. 1975); Fredrick L. v. Thomas, 419 F. Supp. 960 (E.D. Pa. 1976), No. 76-2385 (3d. Cir. 1977); Maryland Association for Retarded Children v. Maryland, No. 77676 (Md. Cir. Ct., Baltimore Co., 1974; Mills v. Board of Educ. of District of Columbia, 348 F. Supp. 866 (D.D.C. 1972); Pennsylvania Association for Retarded Children v. Pennsylvania, 334 F. Supp. 1257 (E.D. Pa. 1971), 343 F. Supp. 279 (E.D. Pa., 1972); In re Reid; No. 8742 (N.Y. St. Commission of Education, Nov. 26, 1973); Pending on the same issue is Crowder v. Riles, No. CA000384 (Super. Ct., Los Angeles Co., Dec. 20, 1976).

126. California Association for the Retarded v. Riles, No. C77-0341 (N.D. Cal., filed Feb. 15, 1977).

127. In re Downey, No. 72 Misc. 2d 772 340 N.Y.S.2d 687 (1973); Kopcso v. Riles, No. 000384 (Cal. Super. Ct., Los Angeles Co., 1977); Kruse v. Campbell, 431 F. Supp. 180 (E.D. Va. 1977); Maryland Association for Retarded Children v. Maryland, No. 77676 (Md. Cir. Ct., Baltimore Co., 1974).

128. Crowder v. Riles, No. CA000384 (Super. Ct., Los Angeles Co. 1976).

129. J. v. Kline, No. 77-2257 (E.D. Pa., filed June 29, 1977).

130. Cloud v. Minneapolis Pub. School, No. 87399 (Minn. Dist. Ct., Hennepin Co., 1977).

131. Donnie R. v. Wood, No. 77-1360 (D.S.C. 1977).

132. Cuyahoga County Association for Retarded Children and Adults v. Essex, 411 F. Supp. 46 (N.D. Ohio, 1976).

133. New Jersey Association for Retarded Citizens v. New Jersey Department of Human Services, No. C-2473-76 (Super. Ct., Hunterdon Co., filed Mar. 16, 1977).

134. Nason v. Carballo, No. 77-C-208 (W.D. Wis. 1977).

135. Tommy P. v. Spokane School District #81, No. 224974 (Wash. Super. Ct., Spokane Co., 1976).

136. Larry P. v. Riles, 343 F. Supp. 7306 (N.D. Cal. 1972); Fredrick L. v. Thomas, 419 F. Supp. 960 (E.D. Pa 1976), No. 76-2385 (3d. Cir. 1977).

137. Pennsylvania Association for Retarded Children v. Pennsylvania, 334 F. Supp. 1257 (E.D. Pa. 1971), 343 F. Supp. 279 (E.D. Pa. 1972); Lebanks v. Spears, 60 F.R.D. 135 (E.D. La. 1973).

138. Colorado Association for Retarded Citizens v. State Department of Education, No. C04620 (D. Col.), as reported in *Mental Retardation and the Law* 3 (December 1975).

139. Mills v. Board of Education, 348 F. Supp. 866 (D.D.C. 1972), as reported in 3 *Mental Health Law Project Summary of Activities* 3 (Summer 1977).

140. Rainey v. Tennessee Department of Education, No. A-3100 (Tenn. Ch. Ct., Davidson Co. 1977).

141. Pierce v. Board of Education of the City of Chicago, 44 Ill. App. 3d 324 (1976).

142. Albrecht v. Tepper, No. H-263 (D. Conn. 1977).

143. Vecchione v. Wohlgemuth, No. 76-2631 (3d Cir., filed Feb. 16, 1977).

144. O'Bara v. Knierim (D. Conn., filed 1976), as reported in 11 *Clearinghouse Review* 2 (June 1977); Rud v. Dahl, No. 77-C-2361 (N.D. Ill., filed June 30, 1976).

145. Bavis v. McKenna, Civ. No. H77-793 (D. Md., filed May 20, 1977). People v. Conley, Ind. No. 2114-76 (N.Y. Sup. Ct., Queens Co.) and People v. Murphy, Ind. No. 2012-76 (N.Y. Sup. Ct., Queens Co.), as reported in 2 *Mental Health Law Project Summary of Activities* #4 (Winter 1976-77).

146. Gish v. Board of Education of Borough of Paramus, 366 A.2d 1337, N.J. App. (1976).

147. Gaylord v. Tacoma School District #10, 559 P.2d 1340 (Wash. 1976). The Supreme Court of the United States refused to review this case in 1977.

148. People v. Burnick, 535 P.2d 352 Cal. (1975).

149. Doe v. Minnesota Department of Public Welfare, No. 142 (Minn. Sup. Ct., Hennepin Co., 1977); Rush v. Parham, No. C76-1445A (N.D. Ga. 1977).

150. Baillie v. Lackner, 702011 (Cal. Super. Ct., San Francisco Co., filed June 22, 1976), appealed to the Cal. Ct. of Appeal.

151. In re Nodvik, Appeal Decision No. B-140782 (Pa. Unemployment Compensation Board of Review, Feb. 15, 1977).

152. Russom v. Nevada Employment Security Department, 20,868 318130 (Nev. Dist. Ct., Washoe Co., filed Feb. 1, 1977).

153. "Sudanese," case reported in the *Los Angeles Times*, Dec. 6, 1977.

154. Chico v. New York City Transit Authority, 21366 (NYS Sup. Ct., filed Dec. 3, 1975).

155. Bavis v. McKenna, Civ. No. H-77-793 (D. Md., filed May 20, 1977).

156. North Carolina Association for Retarded Children and United States v. State, No. 3050 (M.D. N.C. 1976).

157. Ibid.
158. W. Curran, *Failure to Diagnose Battered-Child Syndrome* 296 *New Eng. J. Med.* 795 (1977).
159. Tarasoff v. Regents of the University of California, 131 Cal. Rptr. 14 (1976).
160. Semler v. Wadeson, No. 74-2345/2346 (4th Cir. 1976).
161. Harper v. Cserr, 76-1276 (1st Cir. 1976).
162. Harris v. State, 48 Ohio Misc. 27, 358 N.E. 2d 639 (1976).
163. Voss v. United States, 423 Supp. 751 (E.D. Mo. 1976).
164. Souder v. McGuire, 74-590 (M.D. Pa. 1976); Romeo v. Youngberg, No. 76-3429 (E.D. Pa. 1977); Pettis v. State Department of Hospital., 336 So.2d 521 (La. App. 1976).
165. Donaldson v. O'Connor, 493 F.2d 507 (5th Cir. 1974), 422 U.S. 563 (1975).
166. *New York Times,* Dec. 27, 1977, §L, at 22.
167. e.g., Stone, A. *Recent Mental Health Litigation: a Critical Perspective,* 134 *American Journal of Psychiatry* 273-279 (1977); Halleck, S. "A troubled view of current trends in forensic psychiatry," 2 *Journal of Psychiatry & Law,* 135-157 (1974); Robitscher, J. *Isaac Ray Lectures* delivered at George Washington University (November 1977).
168. Chayes, A. "The role of the judge in public law litigation," 89 *Harvard Law Review* 1281 (1976).
169. Glazer, N. "Should judges administer social services?" 50 *Public Interest* 64-80 (1978).
170. In October, 1979, United States District Court Judge Frank Johnson ordered Alabama's mental health and retardation institutions placed in receivership as a result of noncompliance with the constitutional right to treatment for people confined in such institutions. Wyatt v. Ireland, No. 3195-N (M.D. Ala. 1979).

Chapter 4

Forces Leading to an Alliance

Studies of criminal courts depict not the adversary-trial institution as it exists in myth and movies, but an area in which lower-class clients are hustled through the system just as they are in health care, welfare, public housing, and other meeting grounds of poverty with bureaucracy. . . . Defendants are presumed to be guilty, trials are exceptional, personal characteristics of the defendant and political pressures on the judge, prosecutor, and lawyer count more than evidence, and outcomes are decided more by bargaining than battling.

Lawrence Mohr
Law & Society Review
1976, 10, pp. 621–22

THE CURRENT STATUS OF THE CRIMINAL JUSTICE SYSTEM

The one thing that everyone involved seems to be able to agree upon is that the criminal justice system is in trouble. The problems revolve around the following points:

1. The system is clogged and delays are extensive; too many cases are dismissed; the desire to find dispositions and to "move the docket" overrides all other considerations.
2. The concept of deterrence has very little meaning as things now operate. Arrests are made for only a fraction of the crimes committed; many of the arrests are not prosecuted; and the number convicted and incarcerated is quite small. Whatever is done seems to have little effect upon the crime rate and does nothing good for the individual. There are too many negotiated pleas, and too much disparity and discretion in decisions to prosecute and in sentencing and release.
3. The system's organization is much too centralized, too far removed from citizen involvement, and concerned primarily with meeting the daily work problems of those who work within it.
4. Many of the above problems stem from the criminal justice system's being asked to do too much. Resources are disproportionately focused on minor violations (traffic, conflicts within families and between people known to each other, minor drug and alcohol offenses, etc.), the enforcement of morals, and the administration of social services.

There are other complaints about the criminal justice system, but this outline covers the major problems and provides the background for a discussion of proposed correctives.

REMEDIES

Not surprisingly, consensus ends with the identification of the problems. Harmony with respect to solutions is another matter altogether, in part because it is almost inevitable that solutions to problems at one point aggravate problems at other points. And the choice of tradeoffs is heavily influenced by a person's position in the system and a number of broad ideological forces.

For the most part, the majority of recommendations now being made fall into one of three major categories—the elimination of discretion, decriminalization, and a mixture of unrelated alternatives.

The Elimination of Discretion

I have already referred to the support for determinate sentencing that developed during the 1970s. This movement to eliminate discretion in sentencing and release from prison reflects a shift away from the rehabilitation rationale that has dominated corrections for over a century. It is intended to bring about equitable treatment by assuring that similar offenders get similar sentences for the same crime—a reasonable enough objective. The roots of the movement and the rationale for it have been described in great detail and need not be repeated here.[1] In spite of some expressions of concern, the idea has had popular support from disparate sources, including law-and-order conservatives, prison inmates, and academics. At the time of this writing, at least four states (California, Indiana, Illinois, and Maine) have passed determinate sentencing laws and a number of others are considering such legislation. For several years the U.S. Congress has been considering the adoption of determinate sentencing, and eventual adoption seems probable.[2]

It should be noted that this restriction of discretion is expected to accomplish a number of very different things (hence its appeal to a range of people who can agree on very little else). Some people are attracted to the simple justice and fairness involved in treating all offenders identically—of responding to the act and not the actor. Others are attracted to the deterrent value of immutable penalties and a hoped-for increase in respect that might come to the courts and to corrections systems. Still others lend their support out of a desire to curb the arbitrary use of authority on the part of corrections officials and other members of the therapeutic state, in both the management and release of offenders. Finally, a significant number of people are concerned primarily about the "softheaded" judges and parole boards who are seen as prematurely releasing bad characters who should be confined.

This is a lot of freight for the "just deserts" and determinate sentencing movement to carry—probably much more than it can be expected to deliver. Certainly the proposed changes will have some impact on the problems of the criminal justice system, but it remains to be seen how much of the impact will be curative. Problems can occur at a number of points. For one thing, most critical observers argue that the implementation of determinate sentencing must be accompanied by a reduction in the length of sentences now associated with most offenses. But the public's current mood regarding the crime problem is not likely to lead state legislatures to reduce sentences for most offenses.[3] I noted above that the United States incarcerates more of its people for longer periods of time than any other Western country,[4] and our capacity to expand is limited. But in spite of these facts, the probable short-range result of determinant sentencing will be that more people will serve more time in jails and prisons—an outcome much to be desired in the eyes of some, but clearly not so in the judgment of many others.

A second undesirable outcome of determinate sentencing may be that of simply shifting discretion from one point to another. Although the movement is concerned primarily with disposition (following the adjudication of guilt), it necessarily affects earlier decisions. It is likely that it will lead to more plea bargaining and negotiated settlements in the charging and prosecution phase. Thus we have the undesirable situation where the discretion that is exercised may be less public than it is now. George Denton, Ohio corrections director, says that another effect may be that of transforming discretion from the most qualified members of the corrections department to the lowest paid and least educated. Since the only route to early release is through "good time," the prison guards become the most powerful determiners of the prisoners' future.[5]

But it may be that neither of these outcomes will be realized, for, once again, much of the heat that has been generated appears to be primarily ideological. A critical reading of the "just deserts" movement leads necessarily to the conclusion that discretion is very much alive. Mandatory provisions are not nearly as mandatory as the public or many of the supporters of the movement have been led to believe. Proposed sentencing standards take into account a number of mitigating and aggravating circumstances, such as prior convictions, whether the defendant was a central or a peripheral participant in the crime, and judgments about intent. In addition, most proposals call for 10 to 15 percent off for "good time."

Thus this "major reform" might end up establishing only some minor restrictions on discretion, and in moving discretion to earlier points in the system. From any perspective, it is unlikely that it will have an appreciable impact on solving the existing problems.

Decriminalization

The most effective and rational way to bring relief would be to decriminalize large areas of conduct. Over the years we have expanded our expectations of the courts to include everything from the enforcement of public standards of private morality to the administration of social services. All of this has been done in the absence of demonstrated effectiveness, and at considerable cost. Preoccupation with minor offenses has contributed in part to the limited success in protecting the public from physical harm.

The FBI Uniform Crime Reports reveal that 20 percent of those arrested are involved in crimes without direct victims (drunks, drug abusers, gamblers, and prostitutes).[6] Decriminalization of these offenses would reduce the caseload of each public defender's misdemeanor branch by an estimated 60 percent, with a corresponding effect throughout the rest of the system.[7] Less than 25 percent of the misdemeanor branch's caseload consists of "real" crime—crimes against persons, and property and weapons offenses.[8] Decriminalization would have minimum impact upon the prisons, because there are relatively few people there now who would be covered; but there could be considerable effect on the jail population, and the rest of the criminal justice system.

It has been argued that decriminalization is difficult to bring about because legislatures are reluctant to constrict the purview of criminal law. But there is evidence of some success in decriminalization—e.g., the dramatic change in the management of public drunks; the decriminalization of private consensual adult sexual behavior by a number of states;[9] and the reclassification involved in downgrading the penalties for possession of small amounts of marijuana. It should also be recognized that significant decriminalization has occurred through other than statutory means. Police and prosecutors regularly make decisions not to arrest or prosecute for a given offense, on both formal and informal grounds.

The desirability of further decriminalization is well established—not only for what it could mean for the effective functioning of the criminal justice system, but also in terms of basic rights such as privacy.[10]

There are no obvious drawbacks to such a movement. For those behaviors for which some type of societal response is judged appropriate, disapproval and regulation of behavior could be expressed through civil sanctions, licensing, administrative regulations, etc. Yet at this time there is no reason to expect substantial relief for the problems of the criminal justice system through this route.

Alternatives

This third category of remedies contains a range of procedures and alternatives to the conventional adjudication process. It includes a variety of pretrial intervention programs, "day" fines, work release, community placement, alternative settings for conflict resolution (e.g., neighborhood justice centers), restitution (service, as well as money), victim compensation, an increased role for administrative regulation, license revocation, etc. Some of the proposed techniques are old; others have not been previously tried in this country. A detailed summary of some seventy different alternatives and the central issues relating to them has been provided by David Aaronson and others at the American University Law School.[11] My primary purpose here is to note the growth of alternatives and some of the implications of this growth for the mental health field.

The movement is premised on the following argument:

> It is better to sacrifice formality and dispose of offenders expeditiously and at the earliest stage possible. More speedy, less burdensome and less expensive procedures—so as to reduce trauma and permanent labeling—

must be developed and utilized in the effort to accord offenders their due deserts.[12]

Aaronson and his colleagues found that the therapeutic response to crime problems is very much alive in the development of alternatives, although somewhat blunted:

> The 'rehabilitative ideal' has lost luster, but alternatives do not—as a whole—represent or foreshadow its abandonment. Rather, they indicate a generalized effort to refurbish the ideal by setting more practical and relatively modest rehabilitative goals for ventures into offender treatment through newly christened 'alternatives' and by placing new limitations on the means to be employed by the state in achieving those goals.[13]

The overall thrust of the alternatives movement is disposition centered, with a lessened emphasis on fact finding and the assignment of responsibility. The new approach places a heavy emphasis upon arbitration, negotiation, and mediation in meeting societal ends.

Those who favor the alternatives movement point to a number of potential gains: the avoidance of a criminal record for offenders; the freeing up of resources for more serious problems; an increase in lay involvement; individually tailored sanctions; the avoidance of punishment for those not responsible for their behavior; and increased possibility of taking into account person-environment interactions. This is a rather heady list, and it is not likely that the multiple objectives will be achieved in any given instance. But it is obvious that some of the proposed alternatives will be adopted, with the overall impact on the criminal justice system yet to be determined. Most of the proposals would also increase the opportunities for the involvement of mental health professionals.

THE REASONS FOR INCREASED INTERACTION

Much of what has been said before in this book has in one way or another dealt with the nature and extent of contact between the criminal justice and mental health systems. We turn now to an overview of the forces that are working to expand the points of contact and involvement.

The Dispositional Search

On a day-to-day basis, the central driving force in the criminal justice system is the desire to cut the caseload and to "move the docket." This rule applies to judges, defense, and prosecution attorneys alike:

The lawyer who comes to court expecting the full panoply of due process for his or her client will often feel the judge's wrath. The judges in these courts must function in a system in which correctional facilities are overcrowded, rehabilitation is an acknowledged failure, and judicial incentive is to find a disposition—any disposition. The wise lawyer who practices in these courts is apt to be an expert in arranging access to community mental health services, thus providing judges with dispositions acceptable to the court and least onerous to the defendant.[14]

A recent national study of prosecutors in the United States reveals that 40 percent work alone and that their major concern is the development of methods to cut caseloads.[15] Justice is meted out in terms of a dispositional process rather than an adversarial one, defendants are assumed to be guilty, and the judicial process boils down to a matter of what to do with them through collaboration and negotiation. Court statistics bear this out—less than 10 percent of the cases are disposed of through trial, and up to 40 to 50 percent of all those arrested are dismissed for one reason or another.[16] (This is not a new development. In 1920, sixty-seven out of every hundred arrests for serious crimes in Chicago were dropped by the prosecutor, with similar figures for other cities.)[17] In some jurisdictions one-fourth to one-third of arrests are disposed of through diversion programs.[18]

Defense attorneys also have their problems. Economic factors lead them to prefer the following outcomes for their clients, in descending order of preference:

1. Charges dropped or dismissed early in the process.
2. Dispositions other than adjudication—e.g., diversion to treatment programs.
3. Plea bargains.
4. Acquittal.
5. Reversals on appeal.[19]

This observation is supported by a survey of 3,400 criminal justice practitioners, 61 percent of whom expressed the belief that defense attorneys engage in plea bargaining primarily to expedite the movement of cases. An additional 38 percent agreed that most defense attorneys pressure clients into entering pleas that are unsatisfactory to the client.[20]

Lawrence Mohr has provided us with a general paradigm for decision-making according to one's position in the system.[21] He suggests essentially the following situation:

Judges wish to save time, keep things simple, avoid certain undesirable images, and maintain political favor.

Prosecutors try to maximize production, convictions, and guilty pleas, while avoiding over-leniency in serious cases and earning favorable recommendations from superiors.

Defense lawyers hope to earn a fee quickly (since it usually cannot be large) and keep clients satisfied.

Public defenders are concerned with relieving the time pressure of the caseload, maintaining a good reputation for the office, and obtaining certain resources (e.g., confidence, prosecutorial information).

These courtroom participants understandably do not want to spend much time and energy on routine criminal cases where nothing is really in dispute, and where the costs of gathering information and conducting a trial are almost as great as in serious cases. The same cast of characters meets time and time again, and thus no one wants to defeat other participants badly. All of this leads to a continuing search for accommodation and easy dispositions, with the result that the mental health system is likely to be an increasingly attractive alternative to full processing through criminal justice, particularly for the less serious offenders.

Overlapping Populations

The merger between criminal justice and mental health is facilitated by the similarity of the people being managed by the two systems. On occasion we invoke some rather elaborate diagnostic and sorting procedures—psychiatric exams, psychological tests, and the like—to determine who goes into which slot—the mental hospital, the prison, the institution for the retarded, the institution for the sex offender, etc. But for the most part, this sorting process is crude, unreliable, arbitrary, and only partially related to the condition of the people being sorted. The populations in all of these systems are drawn disproportionately from the poor, from groups with limited education and social competence, and from minorities. Essentially, the same people are moved back and forth between the criminal justice, welfare, and mental health systems. The similarities in population and purpose in all of these institutions has been amply demonstrated by the historians (Foucault for Europe, and Rothman for the United States[22]), and their work changes conditions very little.

Note the following from the current scene. As the mental hospitals have emptied in the 1970s, it has become natural for the prisons to move in some of their charges. This has occurred in Florida, and at the time of this writing, Pennsylvania is planning such a move. I assume that the same thing is happening in other states. Some time ago the state of Minnesota leased a federal prison as a mental hospital, later returning it to be used as a prison. This kind of interchangeability gives credence to Harvey Brenner's recent report that those states with a large prison population tend to have a smaller mental hospital population, and vice versa.[23] It is also interesting to observe that since 1971, community mental health centers have been seeing an increasing percentage and number of individuals who are labeled as "socially maladjusted."[24]

A recent study of the sentencing of sex offenders in California provides further affirmation of the interchangeability of the institutions.[25] It was reported that the judges were not concerned with therapy, but primarily with seeing that the offender received the "going rate" for his or her offense. Thus the mental hospital was used as a sanction between jail and prison; if an offender was returned to court after one year in the hospital, and the "going rate" for the offense was two years, the court tended to add another year in prison. This occurred even when the hospital reported that the patient had been cured or was no longer a problem. Arbitrariness in assignment to prison or hospital was also found in a study of sex offenders in Florida, where the decision was frequently based on contingencies that had little or nothing to do with the basic offense.[26] The President's Commission on Mental Health reported that some jurisdictions seemingly effect prison-to-hospital transfers unilaterally and summarily, treating the transfers as equivalents of administrative "placement and classification" decisions.[27] Such action suggests that the institutions are not seen as radically different.

There is additional evidence that the two systems share the same clients. A California study comparing individuals referred to a mental hospital versus those sent to a jail found very little difference in the behavior of the people, except that, interestingly enough, the more aggressive ones tended to end up in the hospital.[28] If compulsory entry into a mental hospital is made more difficult, it is believed that the people who formerly would have been hospitalized will be forced into the criminal justice system. The following comment is illustrative:

From my own vantage point as a psychiatric consultant to a county jail system, county courts, and the adult division of a county probation department, I believe that . . . mentally disordered persons are being increasingly subjected to arrest and criminal prosecution. They are often charged with crimes such as public drunkenness, disorderly behavior, malicious mischief, or, interestingly, possession of marijuana or of dangerous drugs. Frequently, mentally deranged youth come to police attention because of their disorderly public behavior, and are found to have some marijuana in their possession. Illegal barbiturates are sometimes found on a comatose or groggy person following a suicide attempt or gesture. On occasion, concerned friends or relatives inform police that a mentally disordered person has a stash of marijuana in his room in order to secure his involuntary detention and treatment.[29]

Since we have no direct data on whether the criminal justice system is receiving those formerly sent to hospitals, no firm conclusion can be drawn at this time. But the belief that it is occurring is part of the conventional wisdom of people in both systems.

Some indirect support for the notion that we tend to label a constant proportion of the society as deviant can be found in recent figures relating to institutionalization. Although the population in various types of institutions (mental hospitals, prisons, homes for the aged and dependent, etc.) in the United States changed substantially between 1950 and 1970, the total percent of the population in institutions remained unchanged at 1 percent.[30]

One final example remains of the manner in which troublesome people can be dealt with by either system. Commitments for evaluation for competency to stand trial are generally on the increase. A recent evaluation of criminal commitment to a Massachusetts hospital for pretrial psychiatric examination turned up some interesting findings.[31] Only two out of eighty-seven such commitments for evaluation resulted in commitment to the hospital (72 percent of the cases were dismissed upon return to the court). The authors concluded that this shifting from the courts to the hospital and back reflected a new social policy that has not been explicitly defined: "This unspoken policy involves confinement of social deviants for sequestration and/or treatment under subtle and not-so-subtle coercion."[32]

Similar findings have been reported from the Florida system. The majority of individuals committed as incompetent to stand trial, upon being returned to the court, are continued under the supervision of corrections or mental health.[32] They are moved back and forth from one system to the other for an average of well over one year before final disposition.

It should be noted here that the notion of overlap applies not only to the people being treated or managed in the systems, but also to the people doing the managing. Similar types of professionals and para-professionals are now employed in both settings; in addition to the traditional mental health professionals, they come from a wide range of specialties (occupational therapists, recreational therapists, counselors, special education teachers, etc.). During their careers, individuals comfortably move back and forth from one human service field to another, including corrections and mental health. The argument has been made that the success of expanded partnerships between law enforcement and the mental health system depends on the ability of workers to move freely and effectively between them.[33] Both systems draw from a range of backgrounds, and staff diversity in the mental health system is particularly striking. In a recent report of community mental health centers it was revealed that 72 percent of the total staff time was provided by someone other than psychiatrists, psychologists, and social workers. (Psychiatrists provided less than 5 percent of the total staff time, and one-third of this came from trainees,[34] even though there is an accelerating move towards public service among psychiatrists.[35])

Court Decisions

Chapter 3 contains a detailed review of recent court decisions. At this point we simply need to recognize that the trend is one that will lead to continued interaction between criminal justice and mental health. Across a wide range of settings the courts have consistently required the provision of therapeutic and rehabilitative services. I noted before that even the increase in due process protections, tighter criteria for civil commitment, etc., deal with the circumstances under which the systems relate to one another, with the assumption that there will be continued contact. The newly evolving role of the courts in the administration of social services, and the parallel use of panels of mental health experts, is consistent with the general trend being noted here.

An Escape Valve for Criminal Justice

The mental health system has turned out to be a valuable ally for criminal justice in a number of subtle ways. Prosecutors who do not want to charge a given individual (for any number of reasons) can dismiss the case with the provision that the person receive treatment—frequently of a token nature. In making "humane" or unpopular decisions, judges may use the opinions of psychiatrists and psychologists as a means of sharing responsibility, thus diluting any subsequent blame.

Pleas of mental illness can also be used to achieve objectives not otherwise possible. Take the case of Francine Hughes, Michigan housewife, who in 1977 poured gasoline around the bed of her sleeping husband and then threw in a match. Apparently she was responding to beatings received at his hands over a number of years, and the jury found her not guilty by reason of insanity. She was sent to a mental hospital, but was immediately released as sane. Thus in a situation in which a jury could not find her innocent—there was no question that she had committed the act—mental illness was used as a means of taking into account mitigating circumstances. In essence, it provided a desired way out. (It is worth noting that this has not been a successful route for everyone. There were 132 women in Chicago's Cook County jail last year who reported being abused several times by men they were later convicted of killing.[36])

The courts will continue to need institutions other than prison for offenders who are judged to have diminished responsibility—e.g., those who are severly retarded—and for those with problems that have been successfully labeled as a sickness. We seem to be well on the way to transferring public drunks from criminal justice to other control systems. It is likely that there are other "nuisance" problems that the police would like to see shifted elsewhere.

In short, in the day-to-day functioning of the justice system, the option of turning to mental health for the resolution of troublesome situations is too functional not to be continued and expanded.

The Attraction for Mental Health

The mental health system is more than a passive bystander, waiting to be used. There are good and sufficient reasons for it to seek involvement with criminal justice. For one thing, mental health professionals have no special immunity to the general temptation of all professions and organizations to expand the number and kinds of problems subject to their control. (See page 28.) Recall that one of the first acts by the President's Commission on Mental Health was to increase the estimate of the number of mentally ill by 50 percent. With the continued expansion of the criminal justice system, steadily rising public concern over crime, and a seemingly endless supply of offenders, it is natural for mental health professionals to turn in that direction. Confident of their skills and abilities, it is also reasonable for them to want to contribute to the solution of a pressing national problem.

There are those who would argue that any diversion from the criminal justice system is a desirable thing (except for the obvious need to put away a small, but dangerous, group of offenders). The justification for this is that criminal justice has failed at rehabilitation and creates more deviance than it prevents and that the mental health system is more humane and benevolent, and thus has a better chance of bringing about change. The involvement of mental health is thought to at least soften the sentences meted out by the courts. Even those skeptical about the effectiveness of treatment can endorse the idea that diversion is likely to be a good thing, as it at least avoids the negative consequences of a criminal record. And there is the possibility of learning something about the causes of undesirable behavior in the process of managing offenders.

But the biggest attraction for the mental health system is one of the oldest—money. As funding for criminal justice increased under the Nixon administration, there was an increased interest in cooperative ventures. The director of the National Institute of Mental Health was quoted as acknowledging the lure of the millions of dollars available to criminal justice and the desire to obtain some of those funds for human services.[37] Thus the 1970s saw the beginning of a number of joint programs and projects involving medical procedures, behavior modification, drug and alcoholism treatment, etc. The availability of funds to criminal justice assures a continued involvement of the mental health system.

OVERVIEW

Slowly, and in many instances quietly, the special skills psychiatrists have to offer are being accepted. Police departments, the F.B.I., other government agencies including the State Department, and private groups have shown increasing acceptance of psychiatry and willingness to use the special body of knowledge psychiatrists have to offer.[38]

These words of Peter Bourne, the President's former advisor on health, do not tell the whole story, but they are correct as far as they go. The two systems are slowly, if not quietly, already working together, with all of the evidence pointing toward a further melding. There are too many shared interests, too much of a lobby from both sides, for them not to be more intimately bound. Attention now shifts to another set of questions. How will the continued merger change the operation of each system? What will be the effect upon the individuals being processed? Can we identify the inevitable gains and losses? The legal and mental health systems are invariably portrayed as being in conflict, operating from totally different assumptions about the nature of man, and thus employing different decision rules. Authorities in both camps argue that many of these differences could be eliminated or ameliorated with increased knowledge of the other's expectations and needs. The repeated plea is for tolerance, education, and closer working relations. The journals are full of announcements of conferences on mental health and the law, seminars on psychiatry for judges, etc., and they are well attended. But is all of this necessarily a good thing? In this situation it may be that a certain amount of skepticism and tension is desirable. Is it possible that the individual—and thus society—might be better served if in fact the two systems keep a certain distance from one another? Should their functions remain distinct? Do the losses of amalgamation outweigh the gains?

NOTES

1. See Chapter 1 for references.
2. Senate Bills 1722 and 1723.
3. There is some limited evidence of a willingness to reduce sentences, and increase good-time allowances, primarily in response to overcrowding. See Conrad, J. P., and Rector, M. G. Should we build more prisons? National Council on Crime and Delinquency, 1977, 32–33.
4. Doleschal, E. Rate and length of imprisonment. *Crime & Delinquency,* 1977, January, p. 51.
5. *Time,* December 9, 1977.
6. Cited in Krantz, S., Smith, C., Rossman, D., Froyd, P. and Hoffman, J. *Right to Counsel in Criminal Cases: The Mandate of Argersinger* v. *Hamlin.* Ballinger, 1976, p. 449.
7. Ibid., p. 419
8. Ibid., p. 419.
9. Ibid., p. 455. The U.S. Supreme Court, in a 1978 opinion, upheld the constitutionality of state sodomy laws.
10. For a general discussion of this topic see Kadish, S. H. The crises of overcriminalization. *The Annals of the American Academy of Political and Social Science,* 1967, 157–170.
11. Aaronson, D. E., Hoff, B. H., Jaszi, P., Kittrie, N. N., and Saari, D. The New Justice: Alternatives to Conventional Criminal Adjudication. National Institute of Law Enforcement and Criminal Justice, Law Enforcement Assistance Administration, U.S. Department of Justice, 1977.
12. Ibid., p. vii.
13. Ibid., pp. 40–41.
14. Stone, A. A. Comment. *American Journal of Psychiatry,* 1978, 135, 61–62.
15. Jacoby, J. E. The American Prosecutor: A Search for Identity. National Institute of Law Enforcement and Criminal Justice, Law Enforcement Assistance Administration, U.S. Department of Justice, 1978, p. 7.
16. DeWolf, H. L. *Crime and Justice In America.* Harper & Row, 1975, p. 35.
17. *Chicago Sun-Times,* February 9, 1978.
18. Forst, B., Lucianovic, J., and Cox, S. J. What Happens After Arrest? Publication 4, PROMIS Research Project, Institute for Law and Social Research, 1977, p. 69.
19. Jacoby, p. 13.
20. Krantz, p. 434.
21. Mohr, L. B. Organizations, decisions, and courts. *Law & Society Review,* 1976, 10, 621–642.
22. Foucault, M., *Madness and Civilization,* Pantheon, 1965; *Discipline and Punish,* Pantheon, 1977; Rothman, D., *The Discovery of the Asylum: Social Order and Disorder in the New Republic,* Little, Brown and Co., 1971.
23. Brenner, H. Seminar presented at National Institute of Law Enforcement and Criminal Justice, November, 1977.
24. American Psychological Association *Monitor,* 1978, 9, #1, January, pp. 16–17.
25. Forst et al., p. 129 ff.
26. Monahan, J. Social Power and the Career of a Sexual Offender. Ph.D. Dissertation, Florida State University, 1974.
27. President's Commission on Mental Health. Vol. IV, *Report of the Task Panel on Legal and Ethical Issues.* U.S. Government Printing Office, 1978, p. 1456.
28. Urmer, A. H. *The Burden of the Mentally Disordered on Law Enforcement.* ENKI Research Institute, Chalsworth, California, July, 1973.

29. Abramson, M. F. The criminalization of mentally disordered behavior: possible side-effect of a new mental health law. *Hospital & Community Psychiatry,* 1972, 23, 101.
30. See note 27, p. 90.
31. Geller, J. L., and Lister, E. D. The process of criminal commitment for pretrial psychiatric examination: an evaluation. *American Journal of Psychiatry,* 1978, 135, 53–60.
32. Ibid., p. 58.
33. Beigel, A. Law enforcement, the judiciary, and mental health: a growing partnership. *Hospital & Community Psychiatry,* 1973, 24, 609. Reprinted in J. Monahan, *Community Mental Health and the Criminal Justice System,* Pergamon, 1976, p. 149.
34. National Institute of Mental Health report on community mental health centers. Reported in the American Psychological Association *Monitor,* 1978, January, 9, #1, 16–17.
35. President's Commission on Mental Health, p. 433.
36. *New York Times,* March 10, 1978.
37. Chavkin, S. *The Mind Stealers.* Houghton Mifflin, 1978, pp. 185–189.
38. Bourne, P. G. The psychiatrists' responsibility and the public trust. *American Journal of Psychiatry,* 1978, 135, 174–177.

Chapter 5

Problems with the Alliance and the Renewed Support for Coercion

Ignorance, of itself is disgraceful only so far as it is avoidable. But when, in our eagerness to find "better ways" of handling old problems, we rush to measures affecting human personality on the assumption that we have knowledge which, in fact, we do not possess, then the problem of ignorance takes on a more sinister hue.

Francis A. Allen
The Borderland of Criminal Justice, p. 13

All interventions have consequences, and one of the things we should learn to keep in forefront of our consciousness is that the most important consequences of any intervention almost always turn out to be those consequences that were not intended or planned upon or could not have been calculated beforehand.

Steven Marcus
"Their Brothers' Keepers," in *Doing Good,* p. 66

In addition to whatever benefits accrue from the increased intimacy of criminal justice and mental health, there are inevitable tradeoffs and negative consequences. The objectives of the two systems are not always compatible, and there are costs for the people who work in them, as well as for those they attempt to serve. Some of the potential problems have been mentioned previously, but we turn in the first part of this chapter to a more detailed outline. The second section of this chapter contains a discussion of the extent to which these problems are being ignored and denied in the context of renewed support for coercive treatment in the mental health system.

EXPANSION OF THE NET

Probably the biggest single threat stemming from the availability of diversion and treatment programs is the temptation to place people in them who otherwise would have been released or placed on probation. Evidence is accumulating that indicates that the majority of the people diverted to treatment programs are likely to be minimum risk defendants—people who would have been released or placed on probation in the absence of treatment programs.[1] This is what happens with nearly all first offenders who have not been charged with violent or serious crimes. Norval Morris has given us an example of how this practice of expanding the net would operate for traffic violations.[2] Assume that a policeman has only two options in responding to violators —either to arrest them or let them go. Then provide the officer with a third power—that of issuing a notice to appear. The result will be that fewer will be let go and fewer will be arrested, with a big growth in the new middle category. This seems to be what happens when the criminal justice system has the option of referral to treatment. Also, under a cooperative arrangement with mental health, the prosecuting attorney might be inclined to use the threat of prosecution to induce an offender to accept treatment, and as a means of invoking some sanctions in cases considered too weak to take to trial. In some instances, this might prove to be helpful; it would clearly not be so in others.

I argued earlier that there is good reason to decrease the number and kinds of people under supervision of any arm of the state. It has been widely observed that attempts to intervene in all kinds of minor problems frequently result in greater harm than good. The act of processing people through a system, giving them a label and a self-definition as disturbed, may do more to worsen things than would simply ignoring the problem. This point has been well documented, but let me give just two simple examples. First, a number of studies show that higher levels of surveillance of individuals on probation results in an *increase,* rather than a decrease in recidivism.[3] The second example relates to the provision of protective services for the elderly. In a recent large-scale study it was found that the group receiving such services, in comparison with a control group, had a significantly higher rate of institutionalization and a higher death rate.[4] If the net is expanded (an almost invariable outcome of collaborative work between mental health and criminal justice), we will be providing services in an unknown number of cases not only where they are not needed or wanted, but with negative consequences.

There is yet another undesirable effect that follows expanding the number of people referred to treatment. As referrals are made for minor offenses, and as is often the case, the "treatment" offered is perfunctory and inconsequential, there is a necessary decrease in respect for the administration of the law. The entire process becomes a charade in which there are no winners.

THE WEAKENING OF DETERRENCE

The ascendance of mental health also has implications for deterrence. Although the deterrent value of being processed through the criminal justice system may be limited and subject to considerable debate,[5] it is logical to expect even less as things are turned over to mental health. If offenders are treated as sick and not responsible for their behavior, and if "treatment" is provided away from the public eye, both specific and general deterrence must necessarily suffer. Furthermore, treating the person as sick can have the effect of removing responsibility and decreasing motivation to change the undesired behavior. (This argument is tempered somewhat by the fact that a number of current therapies place a heavy emphasis on the person's assuming responsibility for his or her behavior.) We need to acknowledge that to the extent that compulsory treatment comes to be interpreted as punishment by the recipient (and it certainly is punishment), the deterrent value for that individual could be relatively high. But if the interpretation by the public is that the individual is being "excused" from punishment and not held responsible, then it is reasonable to assume some loss in the general deterrent effect.

INCREASED COSTS

A major argument for the transfer of control from criminal justice to the mental health system is that it will save money. And indeed, for the criminal justice system it may. Early interventions that avoid extensive processing, trials, etc., would obviously conserve resources. But someone must pay for the substitute services, and they can be quite expensive. There are some indications, particularly with respect to public inebriates, that treatment programs often are more expensive than management through criminal justice, and thus the impact of freeing criminal justice resources in this manner has been limited.[6] Furthermore, if the involvement of the mental health system results in an expansion of the net as argued above, then costs can be expected to increase proportionately to the increase in the number of people being processed.

Attempts to assess costs in social programs can get very complicated, and need to take into account not only direct costs, but future productivity, work time lost, the need for public assistance, and a host of similar factors, as well as the ultimate concern for the individual, which could conceivably call for a much greater commitment of resources. But the major point being made here is that the involvement of mental health is likely to be more, rather than less, expensive.

INCREASED HUMANENESS

The argument that the mental health system is more humane than the criminal justice system is open to debate. While it is so in some situations, in others it is not; it depends on the particular settings being compared. Historically, one would be hard put to pick the winner on this issue. For one thing, when there are problems in the mental health system, due process remedies are likely to be less readily available. And although court rulings in recent years have served to increase procedural protection, generally such protections have not been a major concern where the state was presumably acting in the best interests of the individual, and protections have not paralleled those in criminal proceedings.

A case study comparing the "humanity" of a prison versus a hospital can be found in a recent analysis of a Florida situation.[7] Prisoners were moved into vacated units on the grounds of Florida State Hospital at Chattahoochee. Thus the two institutions occupy basically similar physical and political structures. But at that point the similarity ends. The prison units are brightly painted, spacious, furnished with large dressers, rugs, tables, chairs, and decorative plants. The hospital is painted in institutional beige and green, rooms are devoid of rugs and plants, beds are two feet apart, and two patients share four-drawer battered steel dressers. The prisoners have color television, padded couches and chairs, and wooden seats on the toilets. The patients have black and white television, wooden or fiber glass chairs, and no wooden seats on the toilets. The prisoners have spiffy uniforms, fitted and always ironed. Only a portion of the clothes for the patients are ironed; in at least one ward in the hospital, each evening the patients throw their clothes, including shoes, in a pile to be issued another ill-fitting outfit the next day.

Rough and abusive handling of patients was common enough to prompt the hospital to install a videotaping system to monitor the staff. This has resulted in psychiatric aides being fined and indicted on charges of battery.[8]

For all of this the patients or their families are sent bills for up to $812 per month.

Now the hospital at Chattahoochee is not the worst in the country, and it is reasonable to assume that the prison unit is not among the best. And on the whole, it is also reasonable to assume that there is more fear and violence in prisons than in mental hospitals. But this comparison should give second thoughts to those who would assume that a "hospital" setting would uniformly be preferable to a prison.

It is interesting to note that when questioned about this particular situation, the governor and his budget director linked the prisons, mental hospitals, and retardation centers together in commenting, "What all programs want is more. They just want more." Indeed they do.

There is a further point to be considered by those who believe that the prison system is uniformly worse than the mental health system. If our prisons are so bad that diversion to the mental health system is thought to be desirable, then it is time to make the prison more humane. In this regard, John Monahan has commented on the desire of mental health professionals to save as many mentally abnormal offenders as possible from the brutalizing effects of the criminal justice system:

But how can the comparison of mental health personnel be limited to those who are mentally abnormal? If the effects of jail or prison are brutalizing, are they not equally so for the "normal" as well as the "abnormal" offender? Can genuine concern for humane treatment be restricted to those susceptible to diagnosis, when being born in a ghetto is more criminogenic than being "mentally ill"? If community mental health personnel are to remain true to their stated goals of adapting a population perspective and a preventive set, they would do well to redirect their energies from rescuing a relatively few individuals from the criminal justice system to improving that system until it at least reaches a level of psychological neutrality for all concerned.[9]

JUSTICE AND THE AMOUNT
OF TIME SERVED

Another problem lies in the possibility that under the therapeutic system the individual's liberty may be restricted for a longer period of time than would be mandated under criminal law. People have been sent into treatment programs and institutions for indefinite periods, in some instances extending over a number of years. This unfair situation has been documented a number of times within the last fifteen to twenty years, and though much less likely to occur today, it can still happen. This has been particularly likely at institutions such as Patuxent, a Maryland psychiatric prison, where 75 percent of the people committed with a sentence of up to five years served beyond that time.[10] It can also happen in community settings—e.g., apparently some police officers will not take non-skid row public inebriates to a detox center because of the disruption caused by a three-day hold period, compared to the earlier management through criminal justice in which an individual could be released within four hours.[11]

It is also interesting to note that a few years ago the California correctional system, the most "therapeutic" in the country, had the highest rate of incarceration and the largest average stay time.[12]

Additional issues include concern about offenders evading responsibility by feigning mental illness, and the uneven accessibility to psychiatric evaluation as a defense. Such services are expensive, and thus available primarily to the wealthy and the powerful.

Of course it is also true that individuals may get off with lighter sentences by diversion into the mental health system—a favorite subject for newspaper editorial writers. There is widespread concern that offenders are pleading mental illness and gaining release to the community long before they would have under criminal sanctions. But this is probably a rare event that receives disproportionate publicity, since the medical decision rule to err on the side of assuming the presence of sickness and danger leads to generally conservative decisions about release.

There can also be problems of fairness in pretrial diversion in that the process is usually lost from public view. By giving up the opportunity for a full criminal trial, the offender (who has not yet been found guilty) totally surrenders his or her fate to the prosecutor. That decisionmaking is not open and public can lead to the arbitrary exercise of discretion.

ROLE CONFLICT

Not the least of the problems stemming from the amalgamation of the criminal justice and mental health systems concerns conflicts for those working in the latter system. The very structure of the situation raises a number of ethical problems for which there are only limited solutions. Some of these difficulties were illustrated in the discussion of child abuse in Chapter 2, where it was pointed out that the worker might be attempting simultaneously to treat the abusing parent and the child while gathering information for criminal prosecution, and while holding the authority to remove the child from the home. Thus there are multiple clients, and it is anything but clear as to where the primary allegiance lies. The limits of confidentiality are not obvious, and if known, may make effective treatment impossible. Open discussion on the part of the abusing parent may mean loss of the child and criminal prosecution, self-incrimination and a loss of privacy. Failure to engage in open discussion may result in referral back to the court as an uncooperative client, with the consequent sanctions usually associated with such a situation.

Within the last few years the "double agent" issue has surfaced as a major problem.[13] It has been discussed at length in the professional literature, the courts have sharpened the issues by requiring violations of confidentiality, and it has been a subject of concern for those struggling to define relationships which are "just," "constitutional," and "ethical." At this point, the major result of all of this attention seems to be some degree of "consciousness raising"—and a limited degree at that. The mental health professionals' client is said to vary with role and circumstance—sometimes it is the particular patient or prisoner, sometimes it is the administration that pays the salary, and at other times it is the "system" or the community at large. Specific suggestions to deal with these conflicting obligations include such things as (1) informing all parties of the limitations of confidentiality; (2) splitting administrative and therapeutic responsibilities whenever possible within institutions; and (3) purchasing therapeutic services outside of the system. It will be difficult to gain support for suggestions (2) and (3), and although having a prior understanding of the limits of confidentiality is a necessary and minimum requirement, it will not go far in solving the basic problems. Most of the referrals from the criminal justice system require reports on the progress of the offender, the continued threat of criminal sanction, and thus all of the limitations that come from coercive relationships.

Conflicts for the professionals arise also from questions of technology and effectiveness. In many of the contacts between the criminal justice and mental health systems, the questions posed are not answerable with our current knowledge—e.g., the prediction of dangerousness, notions of personal responsibility, the probability of an effective outcome of treatment, etc. Recommendations on these issues have significant implications for the individual (liberty, time served, sanctions or no sanctions), and they are required by the courts, yet many of the professionals involved are aware of the impossibility of validly providing the answers.

This constitutes ethical violations that should be a source of serious concern for the mental health system.

PATHOLOGY VS. CRIME

There are broader implications. When we respond to troublesome behavior by defining it in terms of individual pathology, we deny the political nature of crime and consequently fail to learn from it. For example, if the Vietnam war protesters had been defined as "sick," as suggested by one psychiatrist, then there would have been little need to evaluate the merits of their position. Control through the criminal justice system offers at least a somewhat higher possibility of requiring us to decide through the legislative process what it is that we are willing to tolerate. In the words of Judge Bazelon:

> When proverty, or racism, or crime is labeled a health problem, then society can defer to the experts for its solution, and everyone else is free to go on with business as usual.[14]

When pathology is seen as residing exclusively within the individual, we are not likely to make the social changes that could have a significant impact on crime.

Other problems come with the alliance of the mental health and criminal justice systems, but the major issues have been identified in this outline. We turn now to an examination of the willingness to use the mental health system as a force for maintaining order and the renewed concern for the rights of the family and the "system."

RENEWED SUPPORT FOR COERCION

Paradoxically, in the face of heavy criticism of psychiatry's power abuses, there has been a continued expansion of that power. This is particularly puzzling in light of the depth and breadth of the disapproval that has been expressed since the late 1960s. Much of this criticism has come from within psychiatry, with Thomas Szasz being the most visible and persistent fault-finder.[15] There have been a number of others more centrally associated with the American Psychiatric Association as well—e.g., Alan Stone, Seymour Halleck, and Jonas Robitscher.

Robitscher, the 1977 recipient of the Isaac Ray Award for contributions to forensic psychiatry (given by the American Psychiatric Association), recently devoted the three lectures associated with the award to cataloging the misuses of psychiatric power, the limitations of technical knowledge, and the dangers of psychiatry's unobserved and unchecked entrance into every phase of contemporary living.[16] Yet, following this detailed and critical analysis, he concluded that psychiatry should continue to exercise its power in the courtroom and elsewhere in dealing with difficult social problems. His basic rationale seemed to be that "if psychiatry didn't exist, society would invent it," that someone has to make the tough decisions, and it might as well be psychiatry.

A similar conclusion seems to have been drawn by Alan Stone, Professor of Law and Psychiatry at Harvard, and an officer of the American Psychiatric Association. Stone characterizes his 1975 monograph on mental health and law as dealing largely with failures, and he states that a forceful argument can be made that only modest amounts of effective technical expertise exist and can be provided in the mental health area.[17] Yet, like Robitscher, he seems to favor a continued, if not expanded, exercise of coercive power. Stone lashes out at current legal attacks on the practice of psychiatry and at attempts to gain further legal protections for those subject to the mental health system.[18] He believes that the implicit analogies between psychiatrists and agents of the criminal justice system, and between patients and criminal defendants, are false, and that reforms based on this have been damaging.[19] In coming to these conclusions, Stone ignores an entire body of current literature that shows that flagrant abuses in civil commitment are still common;[20] that the law gets manipulated to achieve desired ends;[21] that the question of mental incompetence to stand trial continues to be introduced overtly to secure involuntary treatment and confinement of deviants under subtle and not-so-subtle coercion;[22] etc.

Stone's proposed solution to reform of the law-mental health system would be found in current federal regulations authorizing Professional Standards Review Organizations (PSROs).[23] The 1972 amendments to the Social Security Act provide for these organizations to promote effective, efficient, and economical delivery of quality health care services under federally funded programs, with the local PSRO intended to be a voluntary association of licensed physicians that would oversee the care provided by each health care practitioner and facility.

This strikes me as a peculiarly naive solution to the kinds of conflict that have surfaced recently in the law-mental health system. Whatever success peer review systems may have had in other areas of medicine, there is not likely to be much carryover into the kinds of problems discussed here. (There is some suggestion that under the cloak of "quality assurance" the PSROs are now being used primarily as a means of cost containment, an early form of medical care rationing.[24]) The basic issues relate primarily to social, and, in the broadest sense of the word, political matters. The criteria employed are as ambiguous and ill-defined as the state statutes relating to civil commitment, and thus leave wide latitude in application. Equally important is that peer review committees of the proposed type tend to function primarily in protecting guild interests, not those of the client. Stone's solution is analogous to the current Blue Cross insurance practice in which allowable fees are established by the physicians who collect the fees, a situation conducive to the exercise of self-interest.

A final illustration of the thinking of nationally recognized psychiatrists can be found in the work of Seymour Halleck. He has written extensively on the social and political aspects of the practice of psychiatry and has expressed concern over the use of psychiatric expertise to obfuscate society's need to develop mechanisms for humane social change. Yet he says that the fears of the therapeutic state are exaggerated.[25] He gives a number of reasons for this belief, including: improved due process protections in civil commitment; a decrease in the number of involuntary patients; legal efforts to stop the use of certain treatments; the organization of ex-patients; and the focus on informed consent. His basic assumption seems to be that psychiatric services are beneficial and that the legal skirmishes take valuable time away from patients. Halleck goes on to say that we may have come far enough in valuing liberty over mental health, and that this belief in the value of liberty may be so powerful that we are neglecting those who need and are likely to benefit from treatment.

My reasons for disagreeing with Halleck about the need for concern over the therapeutic state are spread throughout this book. Specifically, he has more faith in the effectiveness of treatment than seems warranted; he doesn't pay sufficient attention to the informal and covert exercise of authority; he ignores the discrepancy between rights established in law and in practice. Thus Halleck is not unlike Robitscher and Stone in recognizing the problems in the system, the lack of technical knowledge, etc., but at the same time favoring the continued use of coercion. Halleck does meet one major issue head-on when he suggests that mental health values take precedence over liberty. This begins to get close to a fundamental problem. It seems that there is a dark side in most of us that fights against relinquishing power, and enjoys the exercise of power in the name of benevolence. Lionel Trilling says it succinctly:

> Some paradox of our natures leads us, when once we have made our fellow men the objects of our enlightened interest, to go on to make them the objects of our pity, then of our wisdom, ultimately of our coercion.[26]

Francis Allen and Michel Foucault have made similar points:

> Experience has demonstrated that, in practice, there is a strong tendency for the rehabilitative ideal to serve purposes that are essentially incapacitative rather than therapeutic in character.[27]

> Between the latest institution of "Rehabilitation" where one is taken to avoid prison, and the prison where one is taken after a definable offense, the difference is (and must be) scarcely perceptible.[28]

There can be no denial that significant "rights" movements—including consumers', prisoners', women's, welfare recipients', childrens', prisoners', and mental patients'—developed during the 1960s and 1970s. Some observers have characterized all these movements as a revolution of sorts, but the evidence suggests that is an abortive, or at the least, an incomplete revolution. The pendulum swing in the opposite direction is a forceful one, and is reflected in court decisions, the backlash to deinstitutionalization, and positions being taken in professional journals. It is common to hear references to patients "dying with their rights on," to a "lack of freedom caused by mental illness," and to the inappropriate restrictions that prevent "the application of effective treatment."

There is also a renewed fascination with the search for the genetic, organic, and biochemical determinants of behavior. The National Institute of Law Enforcement and Criminal Behavior has started a new research program in this area. Claims of new breakthroughs in understanding and biochemistry of the brain, startingly new discoveries in the limbic system, and new miracle drugs are all being reported regularly. Critics of psychodynamics have a new-found faith that exceeds all promise.[29] Research into all of this should be expanded, but the reports of "breakthroughs" and miracle treatments should be considered in an historical context. It has all been heard many times before, and few of the pertinent studies are ever replicated, or applied to the control of behavior. This is not the place for a detailed review of this topic, but we need to note the significance of this revived interest in the organic and biochemical determinants of behavior. The techniques involved and the language employed somehow seem more "scientific" than that from social and psychological disciplines, and thus easier to justify in application. Since the problems of crime and mental illness are believed to be found within this area, we can justify a lessened concern for social programs and a lessened commitment to understand the political aspects of both subjects.

We now seem to be entering a period when many of the people who have spoken about the abuses in the mental health system are arguing against further reform. And for the most part these people are probably more sensitive to the abuse of power than the average clinicians who have the most contact with clients. At any meeting where issues such as this are discussed it is inevitable that the audience will request more authority to involuntarily hold and treat alcoholics, drug abusers, sex offenders, and the mentally ill. (The willingness to coerce gains moral strength when the individual has broken a law.) When concern is expressed about the appropriateness of coercion, someone always points out that coercion is a given in daily life, and asks questions like: "What is the difference between court-ordered treatment and a husband who goes to a marriage counselor because his wife has threatened him with divorce if he does otherwise? Is one of these situations more involuntary than the other?" Coercion in one form or another is unquestionably a part of the social contract. But I would argue that coercion by the state is of a different order and usually offers a limited number of options. In the situation posed in the question above, the husband does have the choice of getting out of marriage counseling by getting out of the marriage.

A second kind of defense offered for the exercise of coercion by mental health professions can be summed up in the phrase, "that is what the community wants us to do." This is the argument that is frequently used to justify civil commitment,[30] and it is the essence of Robitscher's comment that "if psychiatry didn't exist, society would invent it." Certainly there are some functional aspects to the management of deviance through the mental health system. But the real issue is whether or not this is the most just practice, and whether the exercise of coercion interferes with other values and objectives proclaimed by mental health professionals. The difficulty of combining treatment and control functions is widely recognized, and the one condition common to all forms of therapy is that of mutual trust between client and therapist. The exercise of coercion is not conducive to the development of this trust. The following comment from the Corrections Report of the National Advisory Commission on Criminal Justice Standards and Goals is pertinent:

> In the process of trying to implement this [treatment] model, correctional systems turned to the social work profession for assistance and introduced the caseworker into the penal system to diagnose and treat the offender. This attempt to incorporate casework theory into penal institutions has been warped, however, by a failure to absorb two of the most basic tenets of social work. The first of these is that, for casework to be effective, the individual must perceive that he has a problem and must be motivated to seek help; this is the principle of voluntarism. The second is that the goals of the casework process must be established by the client; this is the principle of self-determination.[31]

One further perspective on the problems that come with attempts to offer treatment to people referred by the criminal justice system has been provided by a professional in a community mental health center. The following is quoted in some detail because it illustrates a number of the problems associated with treating someone on probation:

> . . . an individual seeking the service as a condition of probation will often simply state: 'I was told to come here by my probation office.' If given an appointment, it is quite likely that this client will not show up. If the client does keep the appointment and the mental health professional tries to elicit additional information, one of the following is likely to result:
>
> 1. The client denies having any problems. At the same time, this client will generally show up as frequently as necessary to satisfy the probation requirements.
> 2. While admitting to having a problem, which resulted in an arrest, the client simply states, 'I should have known better.'
> 3. The client bears no responsibility for anything that happened, and sees no connection between anything he did and his legal problems.
> 4. The client comes in regularly, but each time with a different story. While the client is continually lying, because he has a greater investment in 'getting over' rather than 'getting help,' the 'stories' have enough coherence that they make sense.
> 5. The client comes in periodically, generally with an 'explanation' and especially when he is in additional trouble.
> 6. The client comes in sporadically, generally to get out of something else, such as school or work. However, while others may think he is coming regularly, he is generally out doing something else.
>
> Obviously, a clinician cannot provide meaningful therapeutic intervention when a client does not show up, or comes in on a sporadic basis. But even more important is the realization that it is extremely difficult to provide meaningful therapeutic intervention when the client either (a) does not want or (b) is not prepared to accept the services offered.[32]

Stein goes on to say that LEAA studies and conversations with a number of mental health professionals in a number of different clinical settings support his general conclusion regarding the difficulty of success when the request for service is based solely on a judge's or probation officer's directive.

Recognizing this problem, the agency in which Stein works set up a screening procedure. On the basis of phone calls to the probation officer and to the potential client, the desire for service is clinically assessed. "When the client is willing to come in solely to meet the probation requirement or unwilling to come in at all, then we will notify the probation department of this situation and of the client's resistance to the therapeutic process."[33] Unfortunately, this procedure is likely to admit to service only the most verbal offenders and those most likely to be successful in reading correctly the desires of the clinic staff.

The typology outlined above paints a picture of court-referred clients who are less than ideal candidates for therapy—or much of anything else. They are said to deny having problems, to refuse to accept responsibility, to lie continuously, to manipulate the treatment situation, etc. Now it is not possible to say how common this view is among treatment staff, or to what proportion of court-referred cases this general picture would be applicable. But one conclusion seems reasonable: under such circumstances the client is not going to receive much help, either because of deficiencies within the client, or a negative set of expectations on the part of treatment staff that would almost inevitably result in a self-fulfilling prophecy. Not only is help unlikely, but the odds are that the offender will return to court worse off than when he or she left it. When word of treatment failure or "the client's resistance to the therapeutic process" returns to the judge, the outcome is likely to be harsher than it was prior to the referral.

One further comment. My experience leads me to believe that many of the court-referred offenders who state that they came "because my probation officer told me to" are simply being honest. Frequently they have not been told why the referral was made and have no understanding of the kind of services that might be offered. The distance between many of these people and the professional mental health worker is just too great to be overcome without more of an effort than is likely to be expended.

But the major lesson to be learned from all this is the futility of offering "therapeutic services" under coercive conditions. Aside from broader questions about the appropriateness of such referrals, there is good reason to think that the outcome is not going to be favorable in the majority of cases.

The Conspiratorial Point of View

Critics of the mental health system and the alliance of the mental health and criminal justice systems have been described as advocating a conspiratorial point of view. A recent review of Peter Schrag's book, *Mind Control,* is typical:

> Though he says there is 'no conspiracy here, no master plan of control', he writes from a conspiratorial point of view: the powerful against the powerless; the haves against the have-nots. He puts welfare institutions,

universities, hospitals, the drug-manufacturing industry, government at all levels and organized psychiatry on one side, and the poor, blacks, women, children, prisoners and the retarded on the other.[34]

The reviewer goes on to say that Schrag's outrage is dated and has been delivered with greater clarity and more power in fiction. This may well be. But it is debatable whether the concern and outrage is dated. Few people, including Schrag, argue that the abusers act consciously and deliberately; it would be easier to deal with such a situation. The problem is that it is well-intentioned people who tolerate and participate in the abuses, thus creating the continuing need to question and hold up before the public and the professions the harm we do in attempting to do good. Those who doubt this might find instructive the analysis of language employed by the helping professions.[35]

The lessons of the 1970s regarding the relations between government and individuals should not be so quickly forgotten. It was only in 1972 that the U.S. Public Health Service terminated its study of syphilis in which people were deliberately deprived of therapy.[36] Senate hearings in 1977 revealed that the Central Intelligence Agency had been conducting brainwashing experiments on prisoners and the mentally ill without their knowledge or consent.[37] And in spite of the efforts of a new administration, conditions in the mental hospital that produced *Donaldson* v. *O'Connor* has not changed substantially. And so it goes. The defenders of the status quo argue that all social systems are flawed, and that we cannot eliminate them on that basis. Indeed they are. But some can be eliminated. And the subjects of the system can be given a bigger voice as to whether they want the services offered.

NOTES

1. Aaronson, D. E., Hoff, B. H., Jaszi, P., Kittrie, N. N., and Saari, D. The New Justice: Alternatives to Conventional Criminal Adjudication. National Institute of Law Enforcement and Criminal Justice, Law Enforcement Assistance Administration, U.S. Department of Justice, 1977, p. 49; Galvin, J. J., Busher, W. H., Greene, W., Kemp, G., Harlow, N., and Hoffman, K. Instead of Jail: Pre- and Post-trial Alternatives to Jail Incarceration. National Institute of Law Enforcement and Criminal Justice, Law Enforcement Assistance Administration, U.S. Department of Justice, 1977, pp. 71–72; Morris, N. Punishment and prisons, in J. B. Cederblom and W. L. Blizek (Eds.), *Justice and Punishment*, Ballinger, 1977, pp. 160–161.
2. Morris, Punishment and prisons, pp. 160–161.
3. Banks, J., Porter, A. L., Rardin, R. L., Siler, T. R., and Unger, U. E. Evaluation of Intensive Special Probation Projects. National Institute of Law Enforcement and Criminal Justice, Law Enforcement Assistance Administration, U.S. Department of Justice, September, 1977, p. iii.

4. Blenkner, M., Bloom, M., Nielsen, M. and Weber, R. Protective services for older people. Final Report. The Benjamin Rose Institute, 1974, p. 181.
5. National Academy of Science. Deterrence and Incapacitation: Estimating the Effects of Criminal Sanctions on Crime Rates. Study prepared for National Institute of Law Enforcement and Criminal Justice, Law Enforcement Assistance Administration, U.S. Department of Justice, 1977.
6. Aaronson, D. E., Dienes, C. T., and Musheno, M. C. Improving police discretion in handling public inebriates. *Administrative Law Review*, 1973, 460.
7. Ezell, W. Series of articles in *Tallahassee Democrat*, March 19 and 21, 1978.
8. Washington, R. *Tallahassee Democrat*, February 21, 1978.
9. Monahan, J. The psychiatrization of criminal behavior: a reply. *Hospital & Community Psychiatry*, 1973, 24, 107.
10. Chavkin, S. *The Mind Stealers*. Houghton Mifflin, 1978, p. 72.
11. Aaronson, D. E., et al. Improving police discretion in handling public inebriates. p. 470.
12. American Friends Service Committee. *Struggle for Justice*. Hill & Wang, 1971, pp. 91 ff.
13. American Psychological Association, Report of the Task Force on the Role of Psychology in the Criminal Justice System. Washington, D. C., 1978, 9–14; Brodsky, S. L., Ethical issues for psychologists in corrections. Workshop on Corrections, Task Force on the Role of Psychology in the Criminal Justice System, American Psychological Association (Washington, D. C., September 8 and 9, 1977); Burnum, J. F., The physician as a double agent. *The New England Journal of Medicine*, 1977, 297, 278–79; Powledge, F., The therapist as double agent, *Psychology Today*, 1977, July, 44, 46, 47.
14. Bazelon, D. L. Follow the yellow brick road. *American Journal of Orthopsychiatry*, 1970, 40, p. 567.
15. See any of Thomas Szasz's numerous books: e.g., *The Myth of Mental Illness; Law, Liberty, and Psychiatry; The Manufacture of Madness; Psychiatric Slavery*.
16. Robitscher, J. Isaac Ray Award Lectures, George Washington University, November, 1977.
17. Stone, A. A. *Mental Health and Law: A System in Transition*. National Institute of Mental Health, Center for Studies of Crime and Delinquency, 1975, p. 13.
18. Stone, A. A. Comment. *American Journal of Psychiatry*, 1978, 135, 61–63.
19. Stone, A. A. Recent mental health litigation: a critical perspective. *The American Journal of Psychiatry*, 1977, 134, 273–279.
20. Monahan, J. Empirical analyses of civil commitment: critique and context. *Law & Society Review*, 1977, 11, 619–628. Miller, K. S., *Managing Madness*. Free Press, 1976.
21. Warren, C. A. B. Involuntary commitment for mental disorder: the application of California's Lanterman-Petris-Short Act. *Law & Society Review*, 1977, 11, 629–649.
22. Abramson, M. F., The criminalization of mentally disordered behavior: possible side effect of a new mental health law. *Hospital & Community Psychiatry*, 1972, 23, 13–16; Geller, J. L. and Lister, E. D., The process of criminal commitment for pretrial psychiatric examination: an evaluation. *American Journal of Psychiatry*, 1978, 135, 53–60.
23. Stone, A. A. *Mental Health and Law*, pp. 20–21.
24. Burnum, J. F. The physician as a double agent. *The New England Journal of Medicine*, 1977, 297, 278–279.
25. Halleck, S. L. A troubled view of current trends in forensic psychiatry. *Journal of Law and Psychiatry*, 1974, 2, 135–157.
26. Trilling, L. *The Liberal Imagination*, p. 221.
27. Allen, F. A. *The Borderland of Criminal Justice*. University of Chicago Press, 1964, p. 35.
28. Foucault, M. *Discipline and Punish*. Pantheon, 1977, p. 302.

29. For example, see Gross, M. L. *The Psychological Society.* Random House, 1978.
30. Miller, K. S. *Managing Madness,* p. 129-131.
31. Quoted in Banks, J., Porter, A. L., Rardin, R. L., Siler, T. R., and Unger, V. E. Evalution of Intensive Special Probation Projects. National Institute of Law Enforcement and Criminal Justice, Law Enforcement Assistance Administration, U.S. Department of Justice, September 1977, p. 27.
32. Stein, W. M., Jr. Community mental health centers as a criminal justice system resource. Paper presented at the National Conference of the American Society for Public Administration, Phoenix, Arizona, April 11, 1978, pp. 4-5.
33. Ibid., p. 6.
34. *Washington Post,* May 6, 1978, B4.
35. Edelman, M., The political language of the helping professions. *Politics and Society,* 1974, 4, 295-310; Coleman, L. C., and Solomon, T. Parens patriae "treatment": legal punishment in disguise. *Hastings Constitutional Law Quarterly,* 1976, 3, 345-362.
36. Chavkin, S. *The Mind Stealers.* Houghton Mifflin, 1978, p. 12.
37. Ibid., p. 181.

Chapter 6

Safeguards and Short-Term Solutions

The judges of normality are present everywhere. We are in the society of the teacher-judge, the doctor-judge, the educator-judge, the "social-worker" judge; it is on them that the universal reign of the normative is based; and each individual, wherever he may find himself, subjects to it his body, his gestures, his behavior, his aptitudes, his achievements.

Michel Foucault
Discipline and Punish

Will we as a society be able to recognize and respect rights and yet not ignore needs? Can we do good to others, but on their terms?

David Rothman
Doing Good

The movement to divert offenders from criminal justice to a range of alternatives is now well established, and there can be no question of the heavy involvement of the mental health system at all points in the process—pre-trial, trial, sentencing, and corrections. Taking this as a given, and in light of the problems that have been discussed here, we can now move to a consideration of the means of minimizing abuse and restructuring discretion to make its exercise increasingly public and subject to review.

Before turning to specific recommendations, it might prove helpful to bring together and summarize the major themes that have been developed, particularly since the recommendations flow directly from them. I have argued that there is a continuously expanding tendency to medicalize all conflict and social problems, and to turn to experts for solutions. The movement is well advanced, and in the face of arguments to the contrary, the role of the state in providing coerced treatment progresses steadily.

Until now, much of the attention given to the role of the mental health system in criminal justice has focused on institutions, specifically on prisons and mental hospitals. It is important to note that the arena is being shifted from exclusive concern with institutions to the community, where the exercise of discretion and informality is likely to be even greater, where operations will be more covert, and due process will be less likely. As the criminal justice system moves to a range of alternatives, the involvement of the mental health system will increase proportionately.

There are those who argue that sufficient reform has occurred in the mental health system, particularly with respect to legal reform and protections given to those being treated. Our continuing problems are attributed to the need for reform in the courts and the criminal justice system. Certainly there needs to be a renewed concern with applying the law. But criminal justice reform will not suffice. The mental health system has considerable housecleaning yet to be done.

No one would claim that the problems of amalgamation outlined in the last chapter are subject to easy solution. Without some basic change in human nature, the major issues will continue to be a source of controversy and conflict. But some safeguards and checks can be implemented now and at minimum cost. The hope of restraining abuse and restructuring discretion necessarily requires some acceptance of the situation as it now exists. That is, talk of ruling out all contact between the two systems is unrealistic for the many reasons already reviewed. A certain number of features already in place must be accepted as givens. For this reason, some of the recommendations that follow are not internally consistent at every point, but they are attainable objectives, even though in some instances they fall short of what might be desired.

There are four specific propositions that serve as background for the safeguards and suggestions for reform. Although the real head-banging frequently centers on procedure rather than substance, one's view of the reality of the criminal justice–mental health merger is not insignificant, and thus it is appropriate to briefly restate mine. Not everyone will be in total agreement. I can only say that I am led to them by the available evidence, and that in each instance there are a number of people who affirm their reality.

In their day-to-day operations the social control functions of the criminal justice and mental health systems are quite similar. The common wisdom holds that the people in the two systems are in heavy conflict and share a mutual distrust. Close examination suggests that there is more smoke than fire, and that in fact mutual needs and benefits exist.

One authority states that this is the basis for cooperation between the two systems:

> The basis for the collaboration between psychiatry and the law is the fact that they are fundamentally similar institutions that deal with the evaluation and control of human behavior.[1]

A second authority confirms this situation, but notes some minor differences:

> In most of the 50 states, both the police and the mental health authorities are legitimate social control agents. However, the police in all cases have more extensive legal power and can be involved in many more situations of legal intervention than can the mental health worker. Social control via mental health services is real although it is less obvious and circumscribed.[2]

Because it is less obvious and circumscribed, a number of mental health professionals continue to deny this fact, and we have still not shed the fiction that the interests of clients are identical with those of the therapeutic and social service agencies.[3]

Punishment and treatment functions, each independently legitimate, rarely can be successfully combined. There is considerable agreement that a condition of trust between the client and the person offering treatment is a necessity in most instances. This may not apply to the same degree to certain coercive interventions—e.g., psychosurgery, drugs, and some behavior modification techniques. But it would apply in the overwhelming majority of situations involving criminal justice and mental health. Treatment under coercion is likely to result in minimal, if any, gain; and regardless of protests to the contrary, there is a sense in which the mental health professional is always an adversary of the involuntary client. One observer, Ira Glasser, goes so far as to argue that we must begin, at least legally, to mistrust service professionals as well as depend on them, much as we do the police.[4]

Most professionals find it difficult indeed to accept the latter point. They feel that the decisions made are always in the best interests of the client, and they generally fail to appreciate the problems inherent in the benevolence of the state. Evil intent is rare, but conflicting interests, hidden agendas, and a failure to appreciate the operation of personal values is not. It has been suggested that the most disturbing aspect of these situations is that the professional should resist facing these conflicts in the open, so that the hidden agendas have become public only as a result of legal challenges.[5]

The technology of the mental health system is extremely limited. I suspect that most mental health practitioners would not agree with this statement, yet the evidence for its validity is substantial. At best, arguments can be made for the effectiveness of certain behavior modification techniques, and possibly some drugs. Most of what mental health workers are asked to do for the criminal justice system is indeed very poorly done: the prediction of dangerousness, the determination of responsibility, estimates of the probability of successful rehabilitation, etc. The limitations of expertise are acknowledged more readily these days, along with the plea for a more modest role for the expert. The following is an example of a recent statement to this effect:

> . . . simply present to the courts the data we have in precise form rather than drawing legal conclusions. For instance, instead of telling the court, this person is likely to improve if placed in a token economy, professionals should give courts such information in the following type of form: on the average, X% of persons of this sort change in Y, Z specific ways over the time period T. Then the court can decide if that probability of specific change meets the discretionary legal standard of 'likely to improve'.[6]

The problem with even this kind of recommendation is that the specified kinds of information are nonexistent.

Much of the work of the mental health system involves social and moral rather than scientific issues. This follows from the above section, and additional elaboration here is unnecessary. In much of the work within the mental health system, seemingly technical and scientific solutions are offered to essentially moral, social, and philosophical problems. The designation of a given individual as sick (as opposed to bad) is primarily a political act dependent on assumptions of the observer, not the behavior being observed.

RECOMMENDATIONS

The suggestions that follow are not necessarily ordered in degree of importance, and it will be readily apparent that they vary considerably in the level of specificity. Some of the recommendations are essentially guiding principles that imply specific actions not spelled out in detail here. Others are very concrete, with limited intentions.

The overriding goal should be that of providing for only voluntary contacts with the mental health system. The offender should always have the right to refuse referral to treatment and to be processed through the criminal justice system. It is obvious that the threat of criminal sanctions negates the idea of a truly voluntary decision to seek treatment, but this principle would guarantee some freedom of choice. That the concept of voluntariness is complex and not easily confirmed should not stop us from doing what we can to establish it.

This principle goes to the heart of many of the problems discussed in this book, and for that reason will be the most difficult to implement. Only a minority of professionals overtly assert the appropriateness and effectiveness of forced treatment, while a large number of mental health workers, probably a majority, would apply restraints, but leave some room for forced treatment. For example, it has been suggested that when an individual has harmed others, that person no longer has a moral claim not to be changed.[7] This is a reasonable suggestion, and one that would markedly curtail the current level of coercive treatment. Yet the potential abuses, and the inevitable tendency to expand the net, suggest that the wiser choice at this point is to work for the total elimination of compulsory treatment.

There should be maximum lay involvement in decisions relating to the criminal justice system and mental illness systems. If the expertise of the mental health professionals is limited, and if mental health law involves primarily social and moral issues, the role of the expert should be minimal. For example, it makes sense that the attorney and the court can best determine if an individual can assist in preparing a defense. Juries, even with all their problems, may still best determine fairness and justice. The movement towards neighborhood justice systems with proper safeguards may be another helpful reform. And, as has been noted at several points, the turning to experts for the solution of troublesome issues can be an evasion of responsibility. Lay involvement also increases the probability that the decisionmaking process will remain public rather than taking place behind consulting room doors.

The offender should have a much fuller role in decisionmaking than is currently the case. A strong case has been made recently for informed participation as a standard practice in all human services, including the criminal justice system.[8] Since treatment cannot be imposed constructively, success necessarily depends on the active involvement of the person being treated. Thus recommendations to guide the interaction of the criminal justice and the mental health systems should take into account the value of client collaboraton.

There are now the beginnings of an interesting experiment to empower the people in our institutions, rather than simply delivering additional traditional services. This could have a significant payoff.

Relations between the criminal justice and mental health systems should be defined by the due process model of the criminal process. It has been suggested that there are two alternative ways of looking at the goals and procedures of the criminal process—the crime control model and the due process model.[9] The crime control model is characterized by a concern with efficiency, informality, uniformity, and a presumption of guilt. It is an administrative, bureaucratic model that favors extra-judicial practices, and it is the model practiced by the courts. The due process model is that preached by the U.S. Supreme Court. It places a premium on reliability and quality control rather than efficiency, with a presumption of innocence. There are obvious losses and gains with each of these models, but it is clear that the crime control model transfers the sanctioning of authority to the police and reduces the deterrent effect of law. Since this model dominates the system as it now functions, there is a need to place a greater emphasis on the due process model, with the recognition that its implementation will always be limited to some extent. This emphasis is particularly needed in the therapeutic state, where legal protections continue to be less than those within the criminal justice system.

The major court functions currently carried out by mental health professionals should be eliminated: the determination of competence to stand trial, judgments about the degree of responsibility that should be assigned to the offender, and the prediction of dangerousness. The competency to assist counsel in a defense can probably best be determined by the individual's attorney. The latter two functions mentioned in this principle cannot be carried out with sufficient reliability or validity to justify the practice. Recent suggestions that when a mental health professional decides to predict future criminal behavior he or she should be specific and provide the basis for the prediction are not helpful. Increased specificity does not produce knowledge or ability that is nonexistent. Lest this suggestion be considered radical, it should be noted that the President's Commission on Mental Health suggested that mental health professionals should be discouraged from relating clinical findings to questions of who is dangerous, insane, or incompetent to stand trial.[10]

Laws providing for the commitment of sexual psychopaths (and other special categories of offenders) should be eliminated. On the whole, these laws have led to more abuse than good. Needed services can be made available within prisons and the community.

Formal diversion from the criminal justice system should involve a number of safeguards:[11]
 a. *Offenders should be warned of the potential dangers of involvement in a treatment program.* The general tendency in such programs is to overstate the potential benefits and understate the risks involved. Before choosing to enter a treatment program the individual should be informed about restrictions to liberty, the consequences of failing to cooperate or benefit from treatment, the kinds of reports that are to be made to the court, and general expectations in the treatment program.
 b. *The prosecutor should be required to certify that the evidence is such that there is a reasonable expectation of conviction if the case is taken to court.* This kind of certification can easily lapse into a routine without much meaning, but it provides at least a minimum check on the temptation of prosecutors to divert weak cases to treatment programs.
 c. *Diversion programs should be based on written policy that includes reasonably objective criteria for eligibility.* This requirement could reduce prosecutorial discretion and insure some uniformity of application.
 d. *The conditions of deferment of prosecution should be put in writing.* This is an inexpensive and easily achieved objective that merely serves those general purposes for "putting things in writing." It is an extension of the intent to limit discretion and increase fairness.
 e. *Prosecution should not be suspended for more than one year, or for the period of time for which the offender could have been sentenced if convicted.* This is a generous and reasonable limit on the period for which an individual can be threatened with prosecution.

The defendant should have the right to counsel during all phases of decisionmaking. Since the consequences and implications of being placed in a treatment program may be as significant as those stemming from being processed through the criminal justice system, it follows that the protections should be as great. The best way of ensuring this is the provision of competent counsel.

Protections against self-incrimination should be clearly spelled out. Everyone involved needs to know that statements from the offender will not be used in subsequent prosecutions. The ideal way of ensuring this would be through a statutory grant providing the immunity. The client is entitled to know who has first call on the loyalties of the therapist, and under what circumstances that loyalty is not to the client. Since these conditions do not prevail currently, the client should be warned at the outset that what is said cannot be protected and may be used against him. Potential conflicts in loyalty to the client need to be explained and made public.

The waiving of any right (e.g., speedy trial) should be based upon fully informed consent. The need for this requirement should be self-evident, but it is not a part of current practice in many settings. In particular, when a conditional guilty plea is a condition of diversion, this needs to be made clear early in the negotiation process.

There should be provision for a hearing when an individual is to be terminated from a treatment program and returned to court. Significant consequences can stem from being dropped from a treatment program as uncooperative or unable to benefit from treatment. Although the hearing option may rarely be invoked, it should be available.

All of the above rights should be affirmatively communicated to the client, since they have little meaning unless the client is aware of them.

The length of required treatment should never exceed the sentence permissible if the person has been convicted of the crime with which he or she was charged. This was a common abuse in the very recent past, and fairness requires a provision curtailing it.

When treatment is provided in an institution and the defendant is sentenced upon return to court, the time incarcerated should be credited against the sentence.

There should be equality of access to treatment services and access to mental health experts for purposes of preparing a defense. The principle here is that whatever the roles played by mental health experts in relation to criminal justice, the expertise should be available across the board. The application of this recommendation would prevent the common practice of selecting for diversion from criminal justice only these clients who are the easiest to work with, or those most likely to overcome their problems without help. It would eliminate the current situation in which it is usually only the wealthy or those charged with capital crimes who can use mental health professionals to manipulate the justice system.

Mental health services should not be organizationally affiliated with the courts, and when mental health professionals are involved in court procedures it should be on an adversarial basis. Considerable concern has been expressed over the common courtroom spectacle of two professionals taking dramatically opposed positions. Those who are concerned would eliminate this problem by having the mental health expert as an employee or friend of the court. Such a move might cut down the number of instances in which the professionals look foolish, but it is difficult to see how it should contribute to justice. The fact that mental health experts are commonly led to quite different conclusions directly reflects the state of the art. Given this condition, it seems obvious that the truth might best be approached through adversary proceedings. When several conflicting opinions are so readily available, it is difficult to see how justice could be served by having access to only one.

Persons who are being involuntarily transferred to mental hospitals or to psychiatric units in prisons should be granted a hearing equivalent to that involved in civil commitment. Because such transfers can involve a significant change in status, stigma, etc., prisoners should be provided with the same procedures available to nonprisoners.[12]

IMPLICATIONS

Before summarizing the potential impact of implementation of the above recommendations, note should be taken of some things that are *not* being said. I am not arguing that the best response to deviance is always through management by the criminal justice system. I am not denying the existence of a large number of severely disturbed people who are in contact with the criminal justice system, and who need help. Nor am I saying that there is no role for mental health professionals in the criminal justice system—only that the role should be restricted. Services should be available to the individual on a voluntary basis, and it is reasonable to think that mental health professionals possess some knowledge and skills that could be helpful at various points in criminal justice (e.g., the training of police in the management of domestic crisis).

It is important also to recognize the merit of the arguments presented by critics of the move away from the rehabilitation model that in fact treatment has never really been given a chance in our penal institutions, or in most community programs.[13] Finally, because of frequent misunderstandings, I feel the need to repeat that I see no grand conspiracy on the part of mental health professionals to abuse or abridge the rights of offenders under their control. The problems are more subtle than that, and thus in many respects more difficult to control.

The recommendations being suggested here would constitute a large step in the direction of solving some of the problems mentioned in Chapter 5, and in obtaining some of the objectives mentioned in the first part of this chapter.

The import of most of the suggestions is obvious, and there will be costs of one kind or another associated with each of them. For example, there will not be any time savings for the criminal justice system—at least not in the short run. The reverse is more probable. The recommended due process features would involve more court appearances and a somewhat increased formality and structure. Ultimately, there could be a considerable savings in criminal justice resources in that the suggested procedures could hasten the use of alternative solutions, decrease the number of people being processed, and increase the pressure for decriminalizing a number of behaviors. These achievements would come about only over a period of time.

To the extent that the proposals would lead to greater fairness and social justice, there should be a corresponding increase in respect for the criminal justice system.

Offenders would continue to have as much or more of an opportunity for any desired treatment services. They would accrue the benefits of being treated as responsible for their behavior, permitted to make restitution where possible, and allowed to go about their business.

Mental health professionals would be the beneficiaries of increased respect and trust, a well as diminished conflict of allegiances. Less time would be wasted with clients who neither need nor want to be treated, and the interpretation of treatment as punishment would be eliminated. The many hours now devoted to consulting with lawyers, preparing for court appearances, and writing reports for the courts would be freed for other activities. There would be an immediate and dramatic savings of time for the forensic units in mental hospitals in particular.

Finally, the move away from the medicalization of deviance would mean a lessened emphasis on individual pathology, and thus could encourage the search for significant structural change in society.

None of this will be accomplished easily. Resistance can be expected on all sides, if for no reason other than the general reluctance to give up discretionary power, which is clearly what happens as the model shifts from managerial to due process.

Progress has been made in the sense that there is a heightened sensitivity to the problems of amalgamation of the criminal justice and mental health systems. But there is considerable evidence that we are now backing away from these problems, and that whatever new awareness exists has had only a minimum impact on the way the system works on a daily basis. The forces to maintain the existing order are always strong, and guild interests are not likely to support the kind of change needed.

Stanley Brodsky, in discussing the responsibilities and roles of mental health professionals in relation to justice agencies, describes divergent commitments that range from "system professional" to "system challenger":

> A system-professional commitment suggests an acceptance of many existing professional procedures and objectives. While there may be disagreements about the quantity or quality of professional or behavioral science application, there is substantial agreement with existing targets of professional involvement and patterns of belief. On the other hand, persons at the system-challenger end of the continuum suggest that existing functions and loyalties are unjustified or otherwise problematic, and raise questions about the desirability of achieving many of the specified objectives. [14]

Brodsky goes on to elaborate the two polar positions in terms of several areas of responsibility, and he identifies the middle points for each of these. His is a useful analysis that relates to many of the issues raised in this book. I part company with him only when he speaks about effectiveness in changing justice agencies. He is correct in saying that neither the white-coated psychologist who spends his or her day seeing individual offender-clients or the fiery radical concerned only with liberating a few prisoners, has much probability of success. My estimate is that there are comparatively few people at the "fiery radical" end of the spectrum, not many more in between, and a much larger number of professionals at the system-professional end. In the face of a heightened awareness of the problems, there have been few attempts at reform generated among mental health professionals, and these have not met with much success. Most of the effect has been to maintain the existing order.

It may be that a recognition of the problems represents progress of a sort. And it may be that new developments in the social, behavioral, and biological sciences will offer new solutions. But at the moment we are a long way from having a consistent and integrated system of sanctions that incorporates criminal and mental health law.[15] We are obligated to hold continuously in front of us David Rothman's questions posed at the beginning of this chapter:

> Will we as a society be able to recognize and respect rights and yet not ignore needs? Can we do good to others, but on their terms?

NOTES

1. Barton, W. E., and Sanborn, C. J. *Law and the Mental Health Professions.* International Universities Press, 1978, pp. 318–319.
2. Himmelsbach, J. T. Consequences of cooperation between police and mental health services: issues and some solutions. In Robert Cohen et al. (Eds.) *Working with Police Agencies: The Interrelations Between Law Enforcement and the Behavioral Scientist.* Human Sciences Press, 1976.
3. See Gaylin, W., Glasser, I., Marcus, S., and Rothman, D. *Doing Good: The Limits of Benevolence.* Pantheon, 1978, particularly pp. 97–170.
4. Ibid., p. 127.
5. Bazelon, D. L. Psychiatrists and the adversary process. *Scientific American,* 1974, 230, 18–23.
6. Morse, S. J. Law and mental health professionals: the limits of expertise. *Professional Psychology,* 1978, 9, p. 397.
7. Robinson, D. N. Harm, offense, and nuisance. Some first steps in the establishment of an ethics of treatment. *American Psychologist,* 1974, 29, 233–238.
8. Fischer, C. T., and Brodsky, S. L. *Client Participation in Human Services: The Prometheus Principle.* Transaction Books, 1978.
9. See the discussion of H. L. Packer's models in Rossum, R. A. *The Politics of the Criminal Justice System.* Marcel Dekker, 1978, pp. 183–185.
10. President's Commission on Mental Health. U. S. Government Printing Office, 1978, Vol. IV, p. 1481.
11. For a general discussion of some of the points that follow, see Krantz, S., Smith, C., Rossman, D., Froyd, P., and Hoffman, J. *Right to Counsel in Criminal Cases: The Mandate of Argersinger v. Hamlin.* Ballinger, 1976, Chapter XIV; and Aaronson, D. E., Hoff, B. H., Jaszi, P., Kittrie, N. N., and Saani, D. *The New Justice: Alternatives to Conventional Criminal Adjudication.* National Institute of Law Enforcement and Criminal Justice, Law Enforcement Assistance Administration, U. S. Department of Justice, 1977.
12. See President's Commission on Mental Health, Vol. IV, Report, pp. 1456–1457 for discussion of this topic.
13. Silber, D. E. Controversy concerning the criminal justice system and the implications for the role of mental health workers. *American Psychologist,* 1974, 29, 239–244.
14. Brodsky, S. L. (Ed.) *Psychologists in the Criminal Justice System.* American Association of Correctional Psychologists, 1972.
15. See Monahan, J. Social accountability. In B. D. Sales (Ed.) *Perspectives in Law and Psychology.* Plenum, 1977, 241–256.

Bibliography

Aaron, H. J. *Politics and the Professor.* The Brookings Institution, 1978.

Aaronson, D. E., Dienes, C. T., and Musheno, M. C. Improving police discretion rationality in handling public inebriates. *Administrative Law Review,* 1977, 29, 447–485.

Aaronson, D. E., Hoff, B. H., Jaszi, P., Kittrie, N. N., and Saari, D. *The New Justice: Alternatives to Conventional Criminal Adjudication.* National Institute of Law Enforcement and Criminal Justice, Law Enforcement Assistance Administration, U.S. Department of Justice, 1977.

Abramson, M. F. The criminalization of mentally disordered behavior: possible side effect of a new mental health law. *Hospital & Community Psychiatry,* 1972, 20, 13–16.

Adams, S. *Evaluative Research in Corrections: A Practical Guide.* U.S. Government Printing Office, 1975.

Allen, F. A. *The Borderland of Criminal Justice.* University of Chicago Press, 1964.

Allen, H., and Batz, N. Abandoning the medical model: some implications and alternatives. *The Prison Journal,* 1974, 54, No. 2, 4–14.

American Friends Service Committee. *Struggle for Justice.* Hill & Wang, 1971.

American Psychological Association. Report of the Task Force on the Role of Psychology in the Criminal Justice System. Washington, D.C., 1978.

Andenaes, J. *Punishment and Deterrence.* University of Michigan Press, 1974.

Baker, S. H. Court Employment Project Evaluation. Research Design and Implementation. Vera Institute of Justice, December, 1977.

Banks, J., Porter, A. L., Rardin, R. L., Siler, T. R., and Unger, V. E. Evaluation of Intensive Special Probation Projects. National Institute of Law Enforcement and Criminal Justice, Law Enforcement Assistance Administration, U.S. Department of Justice, September, 1977.

Barton, W. E., and Sanborn, C. J. (Eds.). *Law and the Mental Health Professions.* International Universities Press, 1978.

Bassuk, E. L., and Gerson, S. Deinstitutionalization and mental health services. *Scientific American,* 1978, 283, No. 2, 46–53.

Bazelon, D. L. The morality of the criminal law: a rejoinder to Professor Morse. *Southern California Law Review,* 1976, 49, 1269–1276.

Bazelon, D. L. Psychiatrists and the adversary process. *Scientific American,* 1974, 230, 18–23.

Bazelon, D. L. The perils of wizardry. *American Journal of Psychiatry,* 1974, 131, 1317–1322.

Bazelon, D. L. Follow the yellow brick road. *American Journal of Orthopsychiatry,* 1970, 40, 562–567.

Beigel, A. Law enforcement, the judiciary, and mental health: a growing partnership. *Hospital & Community Psychiatry,* 1973, 24, 605–609.

Bernstein, I. N., Kelly, W. R., and Doyle, P. A. Societal reaction to deviants: the case of criminal defendants. *American Sociological Review,* 1977, 42, 743–755.

Blenkner, M., Bloom, M., Nielsen, M., and Weber, R. Protective Services for older people. Final Report. The Benjamin Rose Institute, 1974.

Bohmer, C.E.R. Bad or mad: the psychiatrist in the sentencing process. *The Journal of Psychiatry and Law,* 1976, 4, 23–48.

Bonnie, R. J. (Ed.) *Diagnosis and Debate.* Psychiatric Annals. Insight Communications, 1977.

Bourne, P. G. The psychiatrists' responsibility and the public interest. *American Journal of Psychiatry,* 1978, 135, 174–177.

Borken, J. Review of S. Yochelson and S. E. Samenow, *The Criminal Personality,* in *Federal Bar Journal,* 1976, 35, 241.

Brenner, H. Testimony before the U.S. Congress, Joint Economic Committee, "Social Stress and the National Economy: Recent Findings on Mental Disorder, Aggression, and Psychosomatic Illness." U.S. Government Printing Office, March, 1977, 1–15.

Brodsky, S. L. Ethical issues for psychologists in corrections. Task Force on the Role of Psychology in the Criminal Justice System. American Psychological Association, Washington, D.C., September 8–9, 1977.

Brodsky, S. L. *Psychologists in the Criminal Justice System.* American Association of Correctional Psychologists, 1973.

Brown, B. S. The federal government and psychiatric education: progress, problems, and prospects. Paper presented at the annual meeting of the American Psychiatric Association, Toronto, Ontario, Canada, May 2, 1977.

Brown, B. W., and Courtlers, T. F. "The Mentally Retarded Person in Penal and Correctional Institutions." *American Journal of Psychiatry,* 1968, 124, 1164–69. Cited in M. Kindred, J. Cohen, D. Pennod, and T. Shaffer, *The Mentally Retarded Citizen and the Law.* Free Press, 1976.

Burnum, J. F. The physician as a double agent. *The New England Journal of Medicine*, 1977, 297, 278–79.

Cederblom, J. B., and Blizek, W. L. (Eds.). *Justice and Punishment*. Ballinger, 1977.

Chalfant, H. P. Professionalization and the medicalization of deviance: the case of probation officers. *Offender Rehabilitation*, 1977, 2, 77–85.

Chavkin, S. *The Mind Stealers*. Houghton Mifflin, 1978.

Chayes, A. The role of the judge in public law litigation. *Harvard Law Review*, 1976, 89, 1281–1316.

Civil Commitment of Special Categories of Offenders. National Institute of Mental Health, Center for the Studies of Crime and Delinquency, 1971. DHEW Publication No. (HSM), 73–9017.

Coleman, L. C. and Solomon, T. Parens patriae "treatment": legal punishment in disguise. *Hastings Constitutional Law Quarterly*, 1976, 3, 345–362.

Conrad, J. P., and Rector, M. G. Should we build more prisons? A debate between John P. Conrad and Melton G. Rector. National Council on Crime and Delinquency, 1977.

Conrad, J. P. Corrections and simple justice. *Journal of Criminal Law and Criminology*, 1973, 64, 208–217.

Conrad, P. The discovery of hyperkinesia: notes on the medicalization of deviant behavior. *Social Problems*, 1977, 23, 12–21.

Conrad, P. Soviet dissidents, ideological deviance and mental hospitalization. Paper presented at the annual meeting of the Midwest Sociological Society, April 14, 1977.

Curran, W. J. Failure to diagnose battered-child syndrome. *The New England Journal of Medicine*, 1977, 296, 795–796.

Custer, R. L. The compulsive gambler. *Today in Psychiatry* (Abbott Laboratories), 1977, 3, No. 4, April, 11.

DeFrancis, V., and Lucht, C. L. *Child Abuse Legislation in the 1970s*. American Humane Association, Children's Division, 1974.

Derdeyn, A. P. Child abuse and neglect: the rights of parents and the needs of their children. *American Journal of Orthopsychiatry*, 1977, 47, 377–387.

DeWolf, L. H. *Crime and Justice in America*. Harper & Row, 1975.

Dietz, P. E. Social discrediting of psychiatry: the protasis of legal disfranchisement. *American Journal of Psychiatry*, 1977, 134, 1356–1360.

Dix, G. E. The death penalty, "dangerousness," psychiatric testimony, and professional ethics. *American Journal of Criminal Law*, 1977, 5, 151–214.

Doleschal, E. Rate and length of imprisonment. *Crime and Delinquency*, 1977, 23, 51–56.

Eck, J. An aggregate population dynamics model of the Michigan prison system. University of Michigan, 1977. Mimeo.

Edelman, M. The political language of the helping professions. *Politics and Society*, 1974, 4, 295–310.

Ennis, B. J. Judicial involvement in the public practice of psychiatry. In W. E. Barton and C. J. Sanborn (Eds.), *Law and the Mental Health Professions*. International University Press, 1978, 5–17.

Erskine, H., and Bryant, S. An evaluation of the effect of alcohol-related crime. Unpublished paper, National Institute of Law Enforcement and Criminal Justice, Law Enforcement Assistance Administration, U.S. Department of Justice.

Fersch, E. A. Ethical Issues for Psychologists in Court Settings. Paper presented at workshop on the courts, Task Force on the Role of Psychology in the Criminal Justice System, American Psychological Association, Washington, D.C., May 19–21, 1977.

Fersch, E. A. When to punish, when to rehabilitate. *American Bar Association Journal,* 1975, 61, 1235–1237.

Fingarette, H. *The Meaning of Criminal Insanity.* University of California Press, 1972.

Fischer, C. T., and Brodsky, S. L. (Eds.). *Client Participation in Human Services: The Prometheus Principle.* Transaction Books, 1978.

Fogel, D. *". . . We Are the Living Proof."* The Justice Model for Corrections. W. H. Anderson, 1975.

Forest, B., Lucianovic, J., and Cox, S. J. What Happens After Arrest? A court perspective of police operations in the District of Columbia. Publication No. 4, PROMIS Research Project, Washington, D.C., Institute for Law and Social Research, 1977.

Forst, M. L. *Civil Commitment and Social Control.* Lexington Books, 1978.

Foucault, M. *Discipline and Punish.* Pantheon, 1977.

Fox, R. C. The medicalization and demedicalization of American Society. *Daedalus,* 1977, 106, 9–22.

Galvin, J. J., Busher, W. H., Greene, W., Kemp, G., Harlow, N., and Hoffman, K. Instead of jail: Pre- and post-trial alternatives to jail incarceration. National Institute of Law Enforcement and Criminal Justice, Law Enforcement Assistance Administration, U.S. Department of Justice, 1977.

Gaylin, W., Glasser, I., Marcus, S., and Rothman, D. *Doing Good: The Limits of Benevolence.* Pantheon, 1978.

Geller, J. L., and Lister, E. D. The process of criminal commitment for pretrial psychiatric examination: an evaluation. *American Journal of Psychiatry,* 1978, 135, 53–60.

Gelles, R. Child abuse as psychopathology: a sociological critique and reformulation. *American Journal of Orthopsychiatry,* 1973, 43, 3.

Gillespie, R. W. Judicial Productivity and Court Delay: An Exploratory Analysis of the Federal District Courts. Visiting Fellowship Program Report, National Institute of Law Enforcement and Criminal Justice, U.S. Department of Justice, 1977.

Glasser, I. Prisoners of benevolence: power versus liberty in the welfare state. In W. Gaylin, I. Glasser, S. Marcus, and D. Rothman, *Doing Good: The Limits of Benevolence.* Pantheon, 1978, 97–168.

Glazer, N. Should judges administer social services? *Public Interest,* 1978, 50 (Winter), 64–80.

Greenberg, D. F. Rehabilitation is still punishment. *The Humanist,* 1972, May/June, 28–33.

Grenander, M. E. Thomas Szasz and the right to choose. *Civil Liberties Review,* 1975, 2, 130–140.

Gross, M. L. *The Psychological Society.* Random House, 1978.

Group for the Advancement of Psychiatry and Law. Measure of psychiatry in the criminal courts: competency to stand trial. Report 89. New York, GAP, 1974.

Halleck, S. L., and Witte, A. D. Is rehabilitation dead? *Crime & Delinquency,* 1977, 23, 372–382.

Halleck, S. L. A troubled view of current trends in forensic psychiatry. *Journal of Psychiatry & Law,* 1974, 2, 135–157.

Hiday, V. A. Reformed commitment procedures: an empirical study in the courtroom. *Law & Society Review,* 1977, 11, 651–666.

Himmelsbach, J. T. Consequences of cooperation between police and mental health services: issues and some solutions. In Robert Cohen et al. (Eds.), *Working with Police Agencies: The Interrelations Between Law Enforcement and the Behavioral Scientist.* Human Sciences Press, 1976.

Holden, C. Patuxent: controversial prison clings to belief in rehabilitation. *Science,* 1978, 199 (Feb. 10), 665–668.

Humberger, E. The state and human services: toward a human service rights policy. *Public Administration Review,* 1978, No. 1, January–February, 85–89.

Illich, I. *Medical Nemesis.* Pantheon, 1976.

Ingber, S. Procedure, ceremony, and rhetoric: the minimization of ideological conflict in deviance control. *Boston University Law Review,* 1976, 56, 266–322.

Jacoby, J. E. The American prosecutor: A search for identity. Seminar presented at National Institute for Law Enforcement and Criminal Justice, November, 1977.

Jeffery, C. R. *Crime Prevention Through Environmental Design.* Sage Publications, 1977.

Jeffery, C. R., and Jeffery, I. A. Psychosurgery and behavior modification: legal control techniques versus behavior control techniques. *American Behavioral Scientist,* 1975, 18, 685–722.

Kadish, S. H. The crisis of over-criminalization. *The Annals of the American Academy of Political and Social Science,* 1967, 157–170.

Kapolow, L. E. Patients' rights and psychiatric practice. In W. E. Barton and C. J. Sanborn (Eds.), *Law and the Mental Health Professions.* International Universities Press, 1978, 255–271.

Kassirer, L. B. The right to treatment and the right to refuse treatment—recent case law. *Journal of Psychiatry and Law,* 1974, 2, 455–470.

Kindred, M., Cohen, J., Penrod, D., and Shaffer, T. *The Mentally Retarded Citizen and the Law.* Free Press, 1976.

King, R. The American system: legal sanctions to repress drug abuse. In Inciardi, J. A., and Chambers, C. O. (Eds.), *Drugs and the Criminal Justice System,* Sage, 1974.

Kittrie, N. N. *The Right to be Different: Deviance and Enforced Therapy.* Johns Hopkins Press, 1971.

Krantz, S., Smith, C., Rossman, D., Froyd, P., and Hoffman, J. *Right to Counsel in Criminal Cases: The Mandate of Argersinger V. Hamlin.* Ballinger, 1976.

Lebensohn, Z. M. Defensive psychiatry or how to treat the mentally ill without being a lawyer. In W. E. Barton and C. J. Sanborn (Eds.), *Law and the Mental Health Professions.* International Universities Press, 1978.

Lipton, D., Martinson, R., and Wilks, J. *The Effectiveness of Correctional Treatment: A Survey of Treatment Evaluation.* Praeger, 1975.

Lottman, M. S. Enforcement of judicial decrees: now comes the hard part. *Mental Disability Law Reporter,* 1976, 1, July–August, 69–76.

McGarry, L. A. The holy legal war against state-hospital psychiatry. *New England Journal of Medicine,* 1976, 294, 318–320.

Martin, B. The Massachusetts correctional system: treatment as an ideology for control. *Crime and Social Justice,* 1976, 6 (Fall–Winter), 49–57.

Messinger, S. L. Punishments' troubling future. *Chicago Tribune,* December 16, 1977.

Miller, K. S. *Managing Madness.* Free Press, 1976.

Miller, K. S., Miller, E. T., and Schmidt, W. Diversion of Drug Offenders from the Criminal Justice System—an Evaluation of the Baumgartner Act. Report submitted to the Florida Department of Health and Rehabilitative Services, Drug Abuse Program, 1977.

Miller, W. B. Ideology and criminal justice policy: some current issues. *Journal of Criminal Law and Criminology,* 1973, 64, 141–162.

Mohr, L. B. Organizations, decisions, and courts. *Law & Society Review,* 1976, 10, 621–642.

Monahan, J. Social Power and the Career of a Sexual Offender. Ph.D. dissertation, Florida State University, 1974.

Monahan, J. The psychiatrization of criminal behavior: a reply. *Hospital & Community Psychiatry,* 1973, 24, 105–107.

Monahan, J. Empirical analysis of civil commitment: critique and context. *Law and Society Review,* 1977, 11, 619–628.

Monahan, J. (Ed.). *Community Mental Health and the Criminal Justice System.* Pergamon Press, 1976.

Monahan, J., and Hood, G. Psychologically disordered and criminal offenders: perception of their volition and responsibility. *Criminal Justice and Behavior,* 1976, 3, No. 2, June.

Morris, N. Punishment and Prisons. In J. B. Cederblom and W. L. Blezek (Eds.), *Justice and Punishment.* Ballinger, 1977.

Morris, N. Special doctrinal treatment in criminal law. In M. Kindred et al., *The Mentally Retarded Citizen and the Law.* Free Press, 1976.

Morris, N. *The Future of Imprisonment.* University of Chicago Press, 1974.

Morse, S. J. Crazy behavior, morals, and science: an analysis of mental health law. *Southern California Law Review,* 1978, 51, 526–654.

Morse, S. J. Law and mental health professionals: the limits of expertise. *Professional Psychology,* 1978, 9, 389–399.

Morse, S. J. The twilight of welfare criminology: a reply to Judge Bazelon. *Southern California Law Review,* 49, 1247–1268.

Mullen, J. The Dilemma of Diversion. National Institute of Law Enforcement and Criminal Justice, Law Enforcement Assistance Administration, U.S. Department of Justice, 1974.

Nagel, W. G. On behalf of a moratorium on prison construction. *Crime & Delinquency*, 1977, 23, 154–172.

National Academy of Sciences. Deterrence and Incapacitation: Estimating the Effects of Criminal Sanctions on Crime Rates. National Institute of Law Enforcement and Criminal Justice, Law Enforcement Assistance Administration, U.S. Department of Justice, 1978.

National Association of Attorneys General, Committee on the Office of Attorneys General. *The Right to Treatment in Mental Health Law*, 1976, 46.

National Commission for the Protection of Human Subjects of Biomedical and Behavioral Research, Protection of Human Subjects: Use of Psychosurgery in Practice and Research. Report and Recommendations for Public Comment. Federal Register Part III, May 23, 1977.

National Manpower Survey of the Criminal Justice System. National Institute of Law Enforcement and Criminal Justice, Law Enforcement Assistance Administration, U.S. Department of Justice, no date.

Neier, A. *Crime and Punishment*. Stein and Day, 1976.

Nettler, G. Shifting the load. *American Behavioral Scientist*, 1972, 15, January/February, 361–79.

Nimmer, R. T., and Kranthaus, P. A. Pretrial diversion: the premature quest for recognition. *Journal of Law Reform*, 1976, 9, 208–230.

Page, S. Power, professionals, and arguments against civil commitment. *Professional Psychology*, 1975, 6, 381–393.

Plotkin, R. Limiting the therapeutic orgy: mental patients' right to refuse treatment. *Northwestern University Law Review*, 1977, 72, 490–491.

Policymaker's Views Regarding Issues In the Operation and Evaluation of Pretrial Release and Diversion Programs: Findings From a Questionnaire Survey. National Center for State Courts Publications, No. R001 16 a, April 1975.

Pollack, S. The role of psychiatry in the rule of law. *Psychiatric Annals*, 1974, 4, No. 8, 16–31.

Powledge, F. The therapist as double agent. *Psychology Today*, 1977, July, p. 44, 46, 47.

President's Commission on Mental Health. Vol. I–IV. U.S. Government Printing Office, Washington, D.C., 1978.

President's Committee on Mental Retardation. *The Mentally Retarded Citizen and the Law*. Free Press, 1976.

Progress and problems in treating alcohol abusers. Report to the Congress by the Comptroller General of the United States, April 1977.

Quinney, R. *Class, State, and Crime*. David McKay, 1977.

Reddaway, P., and Bloch, S. Curbing psychiatry's political misuse. *Washington Post*, November 15, 1977.

Redlich, F., and Kellert, S. R. Trends in American mental health. *American Journal of Psychiatry*, 1978, 135, 22–32.

Redlich, F., and Mollica, R. F. Overview: ethical issues in contemporary psychiatry. *American Journal of Psychiatry*, 1976, 133, 125–136.

Reinehr, R. C. *The Machine That Oils Itself: A Critical Look at the Mental Health Establishment*. Nelson-Hall, 1975.

Robbins, I. P. The admissibility of social science evidence in person-oriented legal adjudication. *Indiana Law Journal,* 1975, 50, 493–516.

Robinson, D. N. Harm, offense, and nuisance. Some first steps in the establishment of an ethics of treatment. *American Psychologist,* 1974, 29, 233–238.

Robitscher, J., and Williams, K. Should psychiatrists get out of the courtroom? *Psychology Today,* December 1977.

Rossum, R. A. *The Politics of the Criminal Justice System.* Marcel Dekker, 1978.

Rothman, D. *The Discovery of the Asylum: Social Order and Disorder in The New Republic.* Little, Brown, 1971.

Rovner-Pieczenik, R. *Pretrial Intervention Strategies.* Lexington, 1976.

Rubinstein, R. *The Cunning of History.* Harper & Row, 1975.

Rutherford, A., and McDermott, R. National Evaluation Program Phase I Summary Report. National Institute of Law Enforcement and Criminal Justice, Law Enforcement Assistance Administration, U.S. Department of Justice, 1977.

Satchell, M. A hospital that helps gamblers kick the habit. *Parade,* 1978, January 15, p. 26.

Scheff, T. J. Medical dominance, psychoactive drugs and mental health policy. *American Behavioral Scientist,* 1976, 19, 299–317.

Schrag, P. *Mind Control.* Pantheon, 1978.

Schuchter, A. Child Abuse Intervention. National Institute of Law Enforcement and Criminal Justice, Law Enforcement Assistance Administration, U.S. Department of Justice, 1976.

Schur, E. M. Crime and the New Conservatism. In L. A. Coser and I. Howe (Eds.), *The New Conservatives.* Quadrangle, 1973, pp. 228–242.

Scott, E. P. The right to refuse treatment: a developing legal concept. *Hospital & Community Psychiatry,* 1977, Vol. 28, No. 5, 372.

Scull, A. T. From madness to mental illness. *Archives of European Sociology,* 1975, XVI, 218–251.

Sedgwich, P. Illness, mental and otherwise: all illnesses express a social judgement. Hasting Center Studies, 1973, 1, No. 3.

Shah, S. A. Community Mental Health and the Criminal Justice System: Some Issues and Problems. In J. Monahan (Ed.), *Community Mental Health and the Criminal Justice System.* Pergamon, 1976, 279–292.

Shubin, S. The compulsive gambler. *Today in Psychiatry,* 1977, 3, No. 4, April 1977.

Shwed, H. J. Protecting the rights of the mentally ill. *American Bar Association Journal,* 1978, 64, 564–567.

Silber, D. E. Controversy concerning the criminal justice system and the implications for the role of mental health workers. *American Psychologist,* 1974, 29, 239–244.

Slovenko, R. *Psychiatry and Law.* Little, Brown, 1973.

Sosowsky, L. Crime and violence among mental health patients reconsidered in view of the new legal relationship between the state and the mentally ill. *American Journal of Psychiatry,* 1978, 135, 33–42.

Stein, W. M., Jr. Community Mental Health Centers as a Criminal Justice System Resource. Paper presented at panel on "Law Enforcement and the

Human Service System," National Conference of the American Society for Public Administration, Phoenix, Arizona, April 1978.

Stolz, S. B. (Ed.). Report of the American Psychological Association Commission on Behavior Modification, June 1977.

Stone, A. A. Comment. *American Journal of Psychiatry*, 1978, 135, 61–63.

Stone, A. A. Recent mental health litigation: a critical perspective. *The American Journal of Psychiatry*, 1977, 134, 273–279.

Stone, A. A. *Mental Health and Law: A System in Transition*. National Institute of Mental Health, Center for Studies of Crime and Delinquency, 1975.

Szasz, T. S. *The Theology of Medicine*. Harper & Row, 1977.

Szasz, T. S. *Psychiatric Slavery*. Free Press, 1977.

Szasz, T. S. Letter to the editor, *New York Times*, June 19, 1977.

Szasz, T. S. *Law, Liberty, and Psychiatry: An Inquiry Into the Social Uses of Mental Health Practices*. Macmillan, 1963.

Taborg, M. A., Levin, D. R., Milkmon, R. H., and Center, L. J. Treatment Alternatives to Street Crime. National Evaluation Program, Phase I, Summary Report. National Institute of Law Enforcement and Criminal Justice, Law Enforcement Assistance Administration, U.S. Department of Justice, 1977.

Tapp, J. L. Psychology and the law: an overture. *Annual Review of Psychology*, 1976, 359–404.

Torrey, E. F. *The Death of Psychiatry*. Penguin Books, 1975.

Travisono, A. P. *Prison Crisis*. College Park, Md.: American Correctional Association, 1977.

Urmer, A. H. The Burden of the Mentally Disordered on Law Enforcement. ENKI Research Institute, Chatsworth, California, July 1973.

Van Den Haag, E. *Punishing Criminals*. Basic Books, 1975.

Von Hirsch, A. *Doing Justice*. Hill and Wang, 1976.

Wald, P. Basic personal and civil rights, in President's Committee on Mental Retardation, *The Mentally Retarded Citizen and the Law*, Free Press, 1976.

Walters, D. R. *Physical and Sexual Abuse of Children.* Indiana University Press, 1975.

Wald, M. State intervention on behalf of 'neglected' children: a search for realistic standards. *Stanford Law Review*, 1975, 27, 985–1040.

Warren, C.A.B. Involuntary commitment for mental disorder: the application of California's Lanterman-Petris-Short Act. *Law & Society Review*, 1977, 11, 629–649.

Welsh, J. D., & Viets, D. The Pretrial Offender in the District of Columbia. A report on the characteristics and processing of 1975 defendants. D. C. Bail Agency, 1977.

Wheeler, H. (Ed.). *Beyond the Punitive Society*. Freeman, 1973.

Wildhorn, S., Lavin, M., Pascal, A., Berry, S., and Klein, S. Indicators of Justice: Measuring the Performance of Prosecution, Defense, and Court Agencies Involved in Felony Proceedings. National Institute of Law Enforcement and Criminal Justice, Law Enforcement Assistance Administration, U.S. Department of Justice, Washington, D.C., 1977.

Wilson, J. Q. The political feasibility of punishment. In J. B. Cederblom and W.

L. Blezek, *Justice and Punishment*. Ballinger, 1977.

Wilson, J. Q. *Thinking About Crime*. Basic Books, 1975.

Yochelson, S., and Samenow, S. E. *The Criminal Personality*. Vol. I. *A Profile for Change*. Jason Aronson, 1976.

Yochelson, S., and Samenow, S. E. *The Criminal Personality*. Vol. II. *The Change Process*. Jason Aronson, 1977.

Ziccardi, V. J. Reaction comment to Morris. In President's Committee on Mental Retardation, *The Mentally Retarded Citizen and the Law*. Free Press, 1976.

Zola, I. K. Medicine as an institution of social control. *Sociological Review*, 1972, 20, 487–504.

Index

About the Author

Kent S. Miller was the director of a mental health center for a number of years before becoming a full-time teacher and researcher. He is now Professor of Psychology and Sociology at Florida State University and Director of the Community Mental Health Research Center within the university's Institute for Social Research. His major professional interests relate to problems associated with attempts to control social deviance and, in particular, the role of the mental health system in such attempts. Professor Miller received his Ph.D. in clinical psychology from the University of Texas.